WICKER
FURNITURE
STYLES AND PRICES

REVISED EDITION
with
CURRENT PRICES

ROBERT W. AND HARRIETT
SWEDBERG

Wallace-Homestead Book Company
Radnor, Pennsylvania

Other books by Robert and Harriett Swedberg
  American Oak Furniture Styles and Prices, rev. ed.
  American Oak Furniture Styles and Prices, Book II
  American Oak Furniture Styles and Prices, Book III
  Country Furniture and Accessories with Prices
  Country Furniture and Accessories with Prices, Book II
  Country Pine Furniture Styles and Prices, rev. ed.
  Country Store 'n' More
  Furniture of the Depression Era
  Off Your Rocker
  Tins 'n' Bins
  Victorian Furniture Styles and Prices, Book I, rev. ed.
  Victorian Furniture Styles and Prices, Book II, rev. ed.
  Victorian Furniture Styles and Prices, Book III

Photos by the authors; printing and enlarging by Tom Luse.
Wicker items on the cover from Phillip's Collectables,
The Antique Mall, 110 Fifth St., West Des Moines, Iowa.

Manufactured in the United States of America
ISBN 0-87069-520-7
Library of Congress Catalog Card No. 88–50966

1 2 3 4 5 6 7 8 9 0   7 6 5 4 3 2 1 0 9 8

*We gratefully dedicate this book to Don Brown, whose sense of humor, willingness to share knowledge, and patient guidance helped two aspiring antiques authors start their writing career when he gave their **Off Your Rocker** a gentle push.*

Acknowledgments

The authors are grateful to the following individuals and dealers who gave generously of their time and knowledge to assist us in obtaining photographs and prices for this book. We also wish to thank others who did not wish to be listed.

Antique Emporium, Waukesha, Wisconsin
The Antique Mall (Janet Goetz), Iowa City, Iowa
The Antique Repair Shop (Vic and Anne Durkin), Hammond, Indiana
The Antique Scene (Rachel Cattrell), Moline, Illinois
The Antique Shop (Fred, Doris, Bryan, Shawn, Damon, Darwin Miller), Napanee, Indiana
Antique Wicker & Collectibles (Pat Hill), Cedar Rapids, Iowa
Antiques et cetera (Dale and Jennie Rylander), Altona, Illinois
Attic Antique Shoppe (Pat Koloc), Cedar Falls, Iowa
Bargain Bin (Madge and Mary Foulk), Moline, Illinois
Brick House Antiques (Don and Liz Juhl, Theresa, Dan, Christine, and Sarah), Waverly, Iowa
Donn and Linda Campbell
Churchmouse (Marilyn Johnson), Port Byron, Illinois
Collector's Corner (Michael and Rebecca Dank), Des Moines, Iowa
Connie's Cupboard (Connie Howell), Toulon, Illinois
Lois, Don, Buffy, and Todd Florence
Mr. and Mrs. Edward Gabrys
Grandma's Attic & Wicker Works (Vicki Dahlstrom), Milan, Illinois

Dr. and Mrs. Carl Hamilton
Harman's Bazaar (Georjean and Marvin
  Harman), Iowa City, Iowa
Eleanor Hevalow
Hillside Antiques (Estelle Holloway),
  Frankfort, Illinois
Harold and Betty Hoppe
House of Stuff N' Things (Anna Figg),
  Buffalo, Iowa
Zenola Irving
J & M's Shoppe Collectibles and
  Antiques (Jim and Milly Sawyer)
  Clarence, Iowa
Jane Keeley
Laub's Loft (Myron and Marge Laub),
  Neponset, Illinois
Jim, LuAnn, and Eric Lavine
Kitty and Carl Marshall
Mary Davin's Antiques (Mary Davin),
  Iowa City, Iowa
Alberta and Dick Medd
Dr. and Mrs. Robert A. Nelson
Charles Nute (Booth 103, Webb's Mall
  #2), Centerville, Indiana
Sharon and Dick Olson
Ron and Cindy Phelps
Pleasant Hill Antique Mall (Bill and
  Vivian Yemm), East Peoria, Illinois
Porter's Antiques (Betty and Ed Porter),
  Galesburg, Illinois
Rocky's Antique Mall (Rocky Simonetti,
  prop.), Weyers Cave, Virginia. Also the
  Kentucky dealer at Rocky's Mall
Dorothy M. Roseman
Mrs. Kenneth Rotz
Scrooge and Marley's (Shirley and Ray
  Beasley), Washington, Illinois
Norval and Nedra Smith
Stanley's Antiques, Rock Island, Illinois
The Strawberry Patch (Sharon Parein),
  Cordova, Illinois
Tower House Antiques (Janice Ruland),
  Galesburg, Illinois
Mr. and Mrs. V.B. and Christina
Wanna Buy a Duck (David and Carroll
  Swope), Canton, Ohio
Wilson's Wicker and Weaving (Erma
  Wilson), Cedar Falls, Iowa and
  Country Treasures Mall, Walnut, Iowa
Hal and Betty Zajichek
Henrietta Zerull

Contents

Preface
Wicker Pricing Concepts

In our travels to take pictures for this wicker book, we discovered there was an extreme range in the prices of similar items. For example, a porch swing that needed some repair was priced at $190 in Indiana. A comparable swing, but in good condition, was listed for $800 in an Iowa shop. Similar ranges were repeated for chairs, rockers, and other pieces. Readers might well ask why this occurs.

In an attempt to explain this vast difference, we are going to set up four hypothetical dealer situations and try to indicate how all might arrive at their prices. After you explore these situations, you will better understand why a rocker has a $185 price tag in a Franklin, Pennsylvania, country shop, while an almost identical one is priced at $325 in an antique-decorator shop in Kent, Connecticut. Follow along to a mall in Virginia. You will find a comparable rocker with some damage priced at $75 by a Kentucky dealer who maintains a booth there. Why is the rocker so inexpensive in this shop?

The prices listed in this book are based on the shop tags on the pieces we photographed. Because our project began more than a year prior to the scheduled date of publication, we have added a cost increase percentage to compensate for natural price increases.

In general, the retail price on a wicker article was determined by these factors:
- The original price the dealer had to pay for the item.
- The cost of any repair work necessary.
- Overhead expense when the shop was located outside of the home.
- The dealer margin of profit or markup.

The four hypothetical dealers are classified as follows:

Dealer A: His shop is in his home and he does his own repairs.

Dealer B: Her shop is in her home, but she has to send work out to be repaired.

Dealer C: Their shop is in a rented building, and they do their own repair work.

Dealer D: This shop is in a rented building, and all repair work has to be sent out.

Each dealer has paid the same price for an item. For the sake of simplicity, we will assume that there are no overhead costs for the dealer who works from his home. Also, where overhead is included, it was estimated at the same figure for each store: $30. The next question is: How much does the individual dealer wish to make? Does he want a 50 percent markup? One-hundred percent? The markup on an item is as individual as the dealer.

Using the chair pictured as an example of the article owned in common by the four dealers, let's study the cost chart, which is based on the preceding contrived formula.

Methods of Pricing Wicker

	Dealer A	Dealer B	Dealer C	Dealer D
Original cost of the chair	$50.00	$50.00	$50.00	$50.00
Labor repair costs and/or materials used	12.00 (materials)	65.00 repair	12.00 (materials)	65.00 repair
Overhead	—	—	30.00	30.00
Markup if 50 percent of total dealer cost	31.00	57.50	46.00	72.50
Markup if 100 percent of total dealer cost	62.00	115.00	92.00	145.00
Final price of item at a 50 percent markup	93.00	172.50	132.00	217.50
Final price of item at a 100 percent markup	124.00	230.00	184.00	290.00

This rocker was photographed in a mall. Its Kentucky dealer listed it for **$75.**

If one of the variations in the above chart should change, the price would change accordingly. For example, rent and overhead would be significantly different between small towns and large urban areas and labor costs would differ. A retired person may hand-cane a chair for 40 cents a hole, while someone who repairs furniture for a living may charge 80 cents. Thus the top price could be much higher than the $290 listed in the chart.

By examining the chart, and without any further manipulation of figures, you see that the chair can have a price ranging from a low of $93 to a high of $290.

Dealer A can sell the chair for the lowest price because he does his own work at his own home. He could, if he wished, sell the chair without completing any repairs, make a 50 percent profit, and receive $75 for the chair. He could also decide to increase his margin of profit beyond the 100 percent level. Thus, instead of selling the chair for $124, he could sell it at any price he desired.

The next time you price a piece of wicker furniture, be slow to comment, "That price is low." Conversely, hesitate a moment before you indignantly state, "That's way overpriced!" Remember this chart and some of the factors that must be given consideration. The variation in prices makes a little more sense then.

Look again at the chair discussed in the chart. Here are factors that make it appealing despite its damaged arm and seat.

- Victorian pieces are in demand and this one is circa (about) 1880. Because of its age and attractiveness, it is a salable item.
- It is natural (unpainted) and collectors like natural pieces.
- Chairs are useful. Buyers particularly like rockers.

Here is another chair that is:
- Pre-1880 Victorian with cabriole legs.
- Natural (unpainted).
- Useful.

There is another factor. This is a corner chair, and chairs that angle are not as common as rockers. Collectors like unusual items.

Dealers state that articles such as baby carriages are harder to sell because their use is limited. A new mama or grandmama or a doll collector likes them, but they are less useful to the general public.

Footstools and teacarts seem to be hard to obtain, but sell rapidly. Desks and chairs as sets are fast-movers. Some dealers say it is difficult to find living room suites consisting of settees (sofas), rockers, and chairs to match.

Add another pricing consideration: buyer demand. This can vary in different sections of the country.

Pre-1930 wicker is usually considered collectible. Many dealers shun the tight-machined wicker furniture woven by the Lloyd loom, which was patented in 1917. It utilized man-made fiber.

Additional factors are style, materials used and attractiveness.

Now review the chart and these added points. You can see why it is difficult to price wicker and why such a wide range is possible.

Corner chair in an Iowa shop was priced at **$185.**

1 The Many Faces of Wicker

Wispy wicker whispers. A reed chair creaks and groans its protest when someone sits in it and seems to sigh as it relaxes and readjusts when the sitter arises. Possibly it is this very quality that helps make wicker so comfortable — it is supple. It fits the body's contour, yet provides the support needed for luxury seating.

Wicker is a generic (group) title, not a raw material. This family includes rattan, cane, reed, willow, sea and prairie grass, rush, man-made fibers and other such materials woven to make wicker articles. A description of each follows.

Willow Strong yet pliant twigs (sometimes called osiers) from certain species of willow trees such as the Lemley, purple, and green varieties. Soft, tough, it accepts stain well. Peeled before use. May have slight nubs or knobs where leaf stems grew. Better for open weaving. Twig sizes are not all the same. Despite this irregularity, willow is smooth.

Rattan A tree-climbing, vine-like palm, mainly from the Far East and Southeast Asia. Grows tall, tall and thin, thin. Bends well without breaking. Very strong. Good for outdoor furniture because of its glossy, water-resistant surface. Does not accept stain or paint well.

From rattan come cane and reed.

Willow baby buggy, wooden spokes and metal wheel rims. Label reads, "Philadelphia Baby Carriage Factory—713 & 715 Spring Garden Street, Philadelphia." Dimensions: 51″ long, 23″ wide, 36″ high, **$500.**

Cane Thin strips split from the outer bark of rattan. Glossy on top, fibrous on the bottom so the top side of the thin slice is exposed when woven into seats and backs for chairs. Does not accept stain or paint well. Available in different sizes, the thick cane may be used as a binding to wrap wooden parts such as legs or stretchers.

Rattan hanging wall basket, 8″ wide, 8½″ high, **$40.**

Reed patent (platform) rocker with pressed cane seat and cane patterned back, circa 1880, 22″ arm to arm, 34½″ high, **$475.**

Rattan hanging basket, 8″ wide, 10″ high, **$40.**

Reed The inner part or pith of rattan. Originally considered waste material. First used in 1850s. Accepts stain or paint easily. Very pliant. Slight lengthwise ridges can be seen on it. Comes in various sizes and may be flat, oval, or round.

Swamp reed Not the same as reed from the center of the rattan palm. Grows in marshy places. Various tall, slender grasses used in early times for baskets, thatching and other woven work.

Reed footstool with upholstered inset, 12″ diameter, 9½″ high, **$175.**

Rush hall tree with reed coat hooks, 73″ high, **$245.**

Reed child's rocker (dealer called this German reed), 21″ wide, 26″ high, **$350.**

Fiber (man-made) armchair, 23″ arm to arm, 31″ high, **$150.00.**

Sea grass pie caddy, an unusual, hard-to-find piece, 13″ diameter, 27″ high, **$125.00.**

Rush A perennial plant that usually grows in wet places. The stems and supple leaves of some types are used to make baskets, mats, and other woven objects. Bulrushes are one type so used. Today much rush is man-made of spiral paper for use as chair seats.

Fiber
art fiber
fiber
reed All are names for reed made by machine from treated, twisted paper. Some have a flexible wire core for added strength. It was extensively used during World War I, when shipping was disrupted. Soft and pliable, it was developed in the early 1900s. By the late 1920s this was the most common material used for wickerwork in the United States.

Grasses(dried). Long and strong sea and prairie grasses have a rope-like appearance when twisted and a gossamer feel when used as free strands.

Until man-made fiber was developed, cane and reed from the rattan palm and willow were the most common natural materials from which wicker furniture was made. At times various materials were combined to achieve the appearance that the weaver sought. Less supple material is easier to work into plain weaving, while other types readily adapt to completing intricate designs. Willow, for example, proved to be better for open work, while reed was flexible enough to form a tighter pattern. Prairie grasses were usually wound into strands. When the weaving was done by hand, unusual effects could be achieved. Each piece was individually crafted, and no other item was precisely like it. True, a design could be copied, but there still would be slight variations in the product because man does not stamp out his work with machine precision.

From left to right: round, corded rye grass lidded basket with drop handle, 11″ diameter, 6″ high, **$50**; splint clothes basket, circa 1920, 30″ wide, 19″ deep, 12″ high, **$55**; splint footed egg basket with flat back to hang on barn wall or could stand on feet, 10″ wide, 9″ deep, 11″ high, **$72.50**.

What else makes wicker interesting? It is ancient in origin. From antiquity come stone drawings and carvings that depict people seated on woven furniture. In some cases actual pieces have survived for thousands of years. For example, the Egyptians wove boxes and small, trunk-type chests more than a thousand years before the time of Christ. The dry air helped preserve samples so well that, when archeologists uncovered the sand-buried stone crypts of the pharoahs, they found well preserved wicker sandals, baskets, mats, chests, and stools that had been placed in the tombs with the deceased royalty.

Remember the Bible story in Exodus about baby Moses? Egypt's pharaoh sought to control the enslaved Israelites, who were multiplying rapidly and growing strong. He proclaimed that their newborn males should be destroyed. One Hebrew mother placed her tiny son in a basket fashioned from bulrushes (any marsh plant with slender round or triangular stems) that she had waterproofed with sticky pitch. She placed the basketed infant among the reeds at the river's edge, the pharaoh's daughter found him and decided to raise him as her own son. That small boat-basket, which saved Moses' life, also exemplified early wickerwork.

In England, during Elizabethan times (Queen Elizabeth I reigned from 1558-1603) "twiggie work" was mentioned in literature. This was wicker made from slender, straight, strong, supple willow branches.

Prairie grass, willow, split reed two-deck magazine rack, 14″ wide, 7″ deep, 33″ high, **$150**.

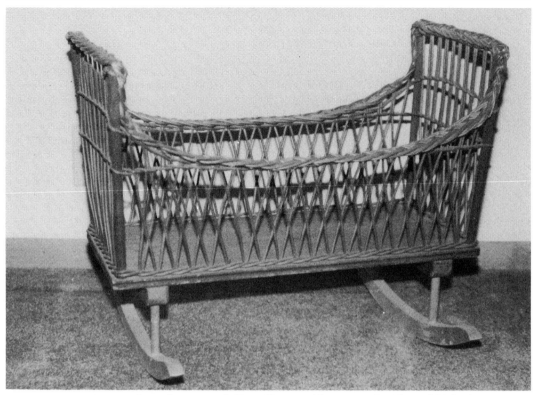

Open weave willow, with reed turning, doll cradle, 23½" long, 11½" wide, 18" high, **$150.**

Reed desk and chair; oak-topped desk with caned side panels and back rail, manufactured by Heywood-Wakefield. Desk: 36" wide, 32" deep, 30" high. Chair: 36" high. **Set, $435.**

Wicker pops in and out of favor. While its roots are in antiquity, it is still being produced currently. Since it is light in weight (except for sofas and chairs with springs and metal supports) it has maneuverability that other furniture frequently lacks. Chameleon-like, it adapts to various settings. It appears comfortably rustic and relaxed on a porch or patio. Conversely, with its delicately woven patterns, it assumes a graceful formality amid aristocratic furnishings. Its naturalness, its history, and its ability to adapt to affluent areas or meager cottages lends wicker an attractive air.

Reed log carrier, used for magazines, 24″ wide, 12″ deep, 18″ high, **$165**.

Reed plant stand, 30½″ high, **$130**.

Salesman's sample office chair with cane seat and natural reed, 16″ arm to arm, 29½″ high, **$275**.

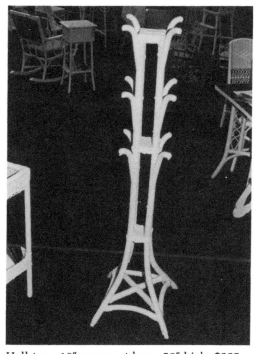

Hall tree, 16″ square at base, 59″ high, **$265**.

2 How to Date Wicker

If you would like to date wicker, the chronology which follows will help. First, consider labels on the furniture. The sequence in the development of the Heywood-Wakefield Company is documented. For others, write to the companies or local historical societies for information. Second, shapes and styles reveal age secrets. Third, materials used yield some clues.

Take labels. For example, the Heywood Brothers and Wakefield Company was not incorporated until 1897. If a chair is marked The Wakefield Rattan Company (incorporated in 1873), it predates this merger. Cyrus Wakefield began operating a Rattan Works in 1855. Unless labels have been tampered with, you know your piece was constructed sometime after 1855, and most probably after the 1873 incorporation, but prior to the 1897 merger. Thus you have ascertained the approximate age of your possession.

Likewise, the same holds true if the name is merely Heywood Brothers and Company. It also predates the 1897 consolidation. A company history states this branch started producing reed and rattan furniture around 1874, thus your chair or other article dates between 1874-1897. Children's carriages were not made until a little later.

If the Heywood-Wakefield Company name and an 1826 date are stamped on a chair, it does not indicate the year of manufacture, but when Levi Heywood first retailed his crafted products. And they were wooden, not wicker.

Music stand with three oak shelves, 19" wide, 15" deep, 25" high. Paper label reads: "Mft. by the Wakefield Rattan Co., Boston, N.Y. & Chicago." Circa 1883-1987, **$325.**

Knowing this will help prevent you from stating gleefully to an antique-hunting companion, "Look, this chair's dated! It's over one hundred and fifty years old!" Instead, you will wisely comment, "Well, this has to be after 1921 because the Heywoods and Wakefields were industrial rivals akin to Ford and Chevy until they merged in 1897. They didn't shorten their name by deleting the word 'Brothers' until 1921. Why, this chair's a youngster." You'll impress others with your expertise.

Armchair, 27″ arm to arm, 42″ high. Paper label reads: "Heywood Brothers & Wakefield Company, Chicago, U.S.A." Circa 1921, **$450.**

Rocker, 31½″ arm to arm, 39″ high. Heywood Bros. & Wakefield Co., Chicago. Circa 1900, **$345.**

Remember that the labels helped establish these facts. Now you realize why you should *save those labels.*

Another change occurred in 1921. Heywood-Wakefield purchased the Lloyd Manufacturing Company. The desk shown has a metal label on the bottom with the Lloyd name only, so it may be assumed it was produced before the new company took over this subsidiary.

The doll carriage pictured was manufactured in or after 1921 since a partial tag on the bottom states: "Baby and Doll Carriages; Furniture; The Lloyd Manufacturing Company (Heywood-Wakefield Co.) Menominee, Michigan." In your search for knowledge, become a sharp-eyed label detective.

Inspect shapes and styles. Since one criterion is not enough to estimate age accurately, study the shapes and styles of wicker. The first American examples

Doll carriage, 29″ long, 29½″ high. Label reads: "Baby & Doll Carriages; The Lloyd Mfg. Co., (Heywood Wakefield Co.), Menominee, Mich." Circa 1921, **$155.**

Kidney-shaped desk, 38″ wide, 24″ deep, 28½″ high. Circa 1917-1921, **$350.**

Photographer's chair, 38″ high. Circa 1890, **$535.**

Label from kidney-shaped desk.

tended to be simple in design, but gradually the Victorian preference for the fancy and frilly prevailed. Note under 1851 in the historical list that exhibits of wicker at the Crystal Palace set styles. The women who attended evidently ohed and ahed over the fanciful rococo designs with their elaborate shells, scrolls, and cabriole legs. They couldn't wait to assign lacy wicker a place in their homes. Many people today share this desire, but do not realize that Victorian wicker is being turned out currently. See Chapter 10 for assistance in how to distinguish the old from the new.

There was some wicker that showed the Art Nouveau influence. Advocates of this artistic concept enjoyed sensuous flowing lines, the languid female figures with long rippling tresses, and objects from nature such as seaweed, long-stemmed flowers, insects, peacocks, butterflies, or seaside creatures. This movement lasted from about 1885 until the late 1930s. The lamp pictured has graceful garlands. These gesso (plaster of Paris bas-relief) flowers are on the shade and flow around the shaft to encircle the base.

Conversely, the stark Arts and Crafts Movement was also an influencing factor in the late 1800s. Devotees disliked tasteless over-mechanization and advocated individual craftsmanship. They rebelled against excessive Victorian ornamentation, and their furniture was purposely crude with a masculine heaviness.

Check 1898. The listing indicates that Mission furniture became the accepted name for the squared, sturdy furniture that was styled and introduced by Gustav Stickley at Grand Rapids, Michigan, displays in 1900. He called his work "Craftsman," but the public termed it Mission. Some suggest Stickley's Craftsman was influenced by the Arts and Crafts Movement. Others say it was so named because it emulated the rough-looking lines of furniture built by missionaries and Indians for churches in the Old West. There are other theories, but one fact remains. His straight, boxy lines replaced the curvaceous Victorian as an American style was born. His wicker combined willow and oak, but he is better known for his oak furniture.

Although diamond shapes woven into wicker actually predate the 1920 Art Deco styles by a few years, Art Deco designs were dominated by geometric shapes — cubes, square lines, and diamonds. On wicker furniture, a diamond pattern was characteristically woven in the back or under the arms of chairs or settees. Frequently it was made more pronounced by being outlined

Floor lamp with rose gesso decoration on base, takes 3 bulbs, 27″ diameter shade, 72″ high, **$625**. Bar Harbor arm chair, club feet, 28″ arm to arm, 34″ high, **$385**.

Basket, 10″ diameter, 11″ high. Circa 1920, **$35**.

Armchair, Art Deco, 30″ arm to arm, 31½″ high. Circa 1920, **$225.**

Baby go-cart, 36″ long, 36″ high. Circa 1920, **$220.**

in color. Cretonne, a heavy cloth with bright huge flowers, was a favorite upholstery fabric used to cover the thick inner-spring cushion seats.

Study the materials listed. You will notice that willow, rattan, and cane sliced from the outer bark of the rattan palm were used at first. Reed, the inner pith of rattan, was discarded as waste. When Cyrus Wakefield discovered that reed was more pliable than rattan and could be painted and stained easily, it soon became more desirable for fashioning wicker than rattan.

In the early 1900s a man-made fiber of twisted treated paper was developed. Since it was difficult to import rattan when warships prowled the seas during World War I, this fiber was utilized instead. It was flexible, easy to work with, and less expensive than the natural materials. It did not require soaking prior to weaving. In fact, it cannot tolerate water. Its popularity was enhanced by the invention of Lloyd's loom, which wove the fiber into sheets that were of the size for standardized prepared frames. Since one loom could do the work of thirty men, Marshall B. Lloyd's invention soon put him in a dominant position in the industry. In order to compete, some firms tried to cut expenses by making loosely woven products that could be fashioned by hand more rapidly than tight ones and required less material. If a chair were woven too loosely, it tended to spread and go out of shape when a person of generous proportions plopped down on it repeatedly. Anyway, style-conscious women preferred the new tight designs for a time; then, since fashion is fickle, the desire for wicker waned.

Despite its contribution to industrial progress, some feel the Lloyd loom with its use of man-made fabric helped bring about wicker's demise. The square lines didn't hold fashion's interest either. When wicker was handcrafted in ornate Victorian fashion, each purchaser had an original. But wicker's stereotyped designs lost favor in the 1930s and remained unappreciated until around 1960. Now interior decorators and magazines proclaim a wicker revival around America.

Significant Dates in Wicker History

B.C. Swamp reeds (various tall, slender grass-like plants) were used to weave articles such as baskets in ancient times. Basket-weaving techniques are basic in the construction of wicker furniture.

1500s As the 1500s ended, the use of wicker furniture had spread to most countries. The American Indians wove baskets and essential utensils centuries before European colonists arrived, but their mode of living did not require furniture.

1620 The earliest known piece of wicker furniture on this continent was brought across the Atlantic Ocean by the Pilgrims. It was a cradle.

1660s The English constructed chairs with woven cane seats and backs. Some were imported into this country and similar ones were constructed here.

1837-1901 The dates of the Victorian Era, the reign of Victoria as queen of England.

1844 Cyrus Wakefield experimented with wrapping wooden chairs with flexible rattan, the discarded material that helped keep cargo from slipping or rubbing and from water damage on ships from China.

Cane is made from thin slices cut from the outer bark of the rattan palm. Chair manufacturers required specific sizes to weave chair seats and backs. Cyrus Wakefield realized hand stripping was costly and time consuming. He made contacts in China and imported the desired strips of cane instead of whole rattan. This reduced expenses, and he became the foremost supplier in the United States.

1840s Levi Heywood invented a machine to bend wood and others to manipulate rattan.

Mr. A. Watkins worked with Mr. Heywood. He invented power looms to weave cane in sheets and a channeling machine that cut grooves so that this prewoven material could be set in them and fastened in the grooves with glue and spline (a triangular shaped reed strip) to form chair seats and backs. This process was quicker and less expensive than caning by hand. Seats made from such webbing are commonly referred to as pressed or set-in cane seats.

1851 London's Great Exposition (held in its sparkling glass Crystal Palace) included an exhibit of Victorian wicker furniture. It revived the 17th and 18th century French rococo designs. Graceful curves, shells, scrolls, and cabriole legs appeared lacy and dainty. A new style trend was set.

1850s Mr. J. and Mr. C. Berrian of New York manufactured wicker furniture with an open weave appearance. They used cane, reed, and willow, which they softened with steam and bent in the desired shapes.

Cyrus Wakefield discovered that the waste inner pith of rattan called "reed" was more pliable than rattan and took paint and stain well, while the outer part of the stalk did not. This reed was used increasingly and soon exceeded rattan in the quantity employed. It is not the same as the grasslike variety that grows in swamps.

By the late 1850s, Wakefield and his inventive associate, William Houston, discovered ways to use waste wicker and shavings to make mats and floor and window coverings.

1855   Cyrus Wakefield established a Rattan Works in South Reading, Massachusetts, and, at first, skirt hoops and baskets were made. He began stripping cane from imported rattan for woven chair seats and backs, but the hand labor was too expensive. This caused Wakefield to invent machines that divided the outside surface of the rattan into strands of the desired sizes. These were shaved smoothly, tied in bunches containing one thousand feet, bleached, bundled, and sold. By 1873, the plant employed more than a thousand workers. Mats, baskets, chairs, cradles, cribs, sofas, baby carriages, window shades, brushes, wall and fire screens, wall pockets, slipper holders, clothes beaters, as well as rattan whips, umbrellas, corsets, and saddles, were among the many articles manufactured.

1861   Levi Heywood, who first made and sold wooden chairs in 1826, founded a company in Gardner, Massachusetts. The company produced bentwoods and Windsors predominately and became the largest chair factory in America by 1870. The founding date is considered to be 1826 and it may be stamped on pieces marketed by the Heywood-Wakefield Company in the 1900s.

1865-   Wicker furniture was popular,
1880   especially in out-of-door settings.

1868   South Reading, Massachusetts, was renamed Wakefield in honor of Cyrus, the town philanthropist.

1870   William Houston invented a loom to weave cane webbing, which was later used for railroad and streetcar seats.

By 1870, water power, soon followed by steam, began replacing hand power in factories.

1873   The Wakefield Rattan Company was incorporated and when Cyrus died shortly thereafter, his nephew, Cyrus II, took over the business.

1874   Heywood Brothers and Company began making reed and rattan furniture.

1875   The American Rattan Company at Fitchburg, Massachusetts, was one of the oldest rattan companies in America. Levi Heywood was one of the original stockholders. Cyrus Wakefield II bought this competitor and other small rattan companies.

1880s   Reed replaced rattan as the most commonly used material for wicker furniture. Montgomery Ward Company and Sears, Roebuck and Company offered less expensive wicker to the public through their mail order catalogs.

1882   Levi Heywood died.

1897   The rival companies merged to become Heywood Brothers and Wakefield Company and grew to become the largest producers of wicker furniture in the world.

1898   Gustav Stickley developed a bulky, "Craftsman" furniture, the first distinct native United States style. He contended that homes and furnishings should be compatible and help set the moral tone for family living. Others copied his ideas and the common name for this strong, straight furniture was "mission." By 1910-15 Victorian and Art Nouveau flowing lines and curves in wicker furniture became passé as the rectangular Mission styles took over. Gustav Stickley made wicker of willow despite the fact that oak furniture was his specialty.

Early 1900s A fiber was made from twisted, treated paper that was sometimes strengthened by wrapping it around a flexible wire core. It was also referred to as art fiber or fiber reed, or spelled fibre. It came into extensive use during World War I.

1906 Marshall B. Lloyd, inventor and baby buggy maker, moved his plant to Menominee, Michigan.

1917 Marshall B. Lloyd invented a loom to weave the less costly and more pliable fiber (man-made) into material that could be applied to frames constructed separately. The machine could do the work thirty times faster than a man could by hand. Lloyd's business soon dominated the industry.

1921 Heywood-Wakefield Company (the name was simplified from the original merger) bought the Lloyd Manufacturing Company.

1920s Art Deco wicker furniture frequently featured a woven diamond design and square functional lines. Innerspring seats were the norm. About 80 percent of wicker furniture was constructed from man-made fiber by the late 1920s.

1927 Charles A. Lindbergh completed the first non-stop solo flight across the Atlantic Ocean in "The Spirit of St. Louis," which had a pilot's seat made of light wicker. Natural materials were lighter than man-made fiber for airplane seats.

1930s Wicker furniture gradually went out of style.

1960s The interest in wicker furniture revived. The ornate curved lines of the Victorian versions are especially desirable. Purists prefer the natural to the painted product. The later rectangular furniture, constructed of man-made fiber with a tight machined weave, is less expensive.

1979 The Wood Furniture Division of Heywood-Wakefield and its Historical Department closed in 1979. No further information could be obtained. But the company produced furniture for 153 years.

A special thank you is extended to William E. Jones, assistant curator of the Wakefield Historical Society, Wakefield, Massachusetts, for making suggestions. He provided additional information from Lilley Eaton's *History of Reading, Massachusetts,* published in 1874, and *A Completed Century (1826-1926) — The Story of the Heywood-Wakefield Co.,* published by the Heywood-Wakefield firm in 1926.

3 Wicker for the Wee Willie Winkie Set

Wicker has long catered to the nursery age group, with charming results. As stated in Chapter 2, the first known example of wicker furniture on this continent was a child's item. William and Susanna White were anticipating the arrival of a baby when they boarded the *Mayflower* in 1620. It is thought they brought along a wicker cradle. A letter from the Pilgrim Society, Plymouth, Massachusetts, states, "Peregrine White was born aboard the *Mayflower* while the ship was off what is now Provincetown, Massachusetts, while the Pilgrims were exploring the area. Peregrine was a male who lived until 1704. The wicker cradle in our possession is identified as the White Family cradle."

When William Bradford, the second governor of Plymouth, wrote a history of the Pilgrims, he listed the one hundred and two who disembarked at Plymouth Rock. Among the names in Bradford's own words, and 17th century spelling, were "Mr. William White, and Susana, his wife, and one sone caled Resolved, and one borne a shipbord, caled Peregriene . . ." The Governor's spelling is slightly different from that found in the Pilgrim Society records, but the White cradle is carefully preserved as part of America's heritage. Peregrine was the first child of Pilgrim parentage born in America.

Woven cribs, cradles, and bassinets provided safe sleeping spots for infants.

When mobility was a consideration, go-carts and baby carriages were available in

Baby bassinet, 37" wide, 20¼" deep, 43" high. Circa 1930, **$175.**

various styles and prices. Old advertisements referred to reed, not wicker, products. A replica of the Sear's, Roebuck Catalogue for 1897 featured a stylish carriage with a scalloped edge. If parents wanted to assure a gentle ride for their offspring, rubber tires could be added to the steel wheels for an extra dollar. A new development was the adjustable buggy hood, which could be moved to protect baby from the wind and sun. When it was not required, it could be taken off. Chelsea

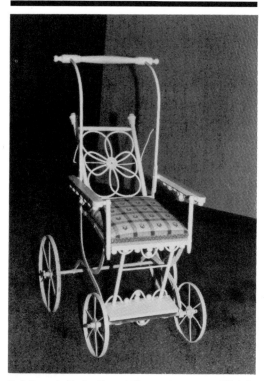

Folding doll stroller, 12″ arm to arm, 26″ high, **$275.**

Doll Stroller, 28″ long, 9″ deep, 23½″ high, **$275.**

House Publishers of New York put out this reproduction catalog, and it is a learning experience to look through it.

Folding go-carts with adjustable reclining features were new in the early 1900s. The Gun Digest Company of Chicago republished a 1908 Sears, Roebuck & Co. catalog that is fascinating to examine. An ad writer appeared confused when he announced that upholstered go-carts were made to order, a task that required three to six days to complete. The next line stated that the supplier's contract promised delivery within eight days. However, usually an order only took two or three days to fill. These conflicting time schedules must have confused would-be buyers. Upholstery material offered in various colors ranged from sturdy denim to silk damask. No go-cart pictured is collapsible, but the shape of these predecessors of the stroller can be seen. The footrest was called "the dash."

Go-cart, 25″ long, 9″ deep, 26″ high. Advertisement called this a go-cart in the March, 1899, *Ladies' Home Journal*, and it sold for $2.50 to $20. As pictured, **$375.**

17

Baby go-cart, 27″ wheel to wheel, 18″ deep, 33″ high. Woven cane, metal spoke wheels, braid on arms. Circa 1900, **$165.**

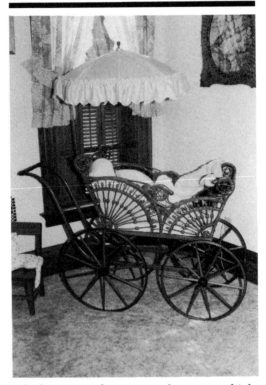

Baby buggy, 52″ long, 16½″ deep, 56½″ high. Metal wheels with wooden spokes. Circa late 1800s, **$775.**

High-wheel doll buggy, braided edge, pin-striped wheels; original paint with leather and velvet upholstery; 40″ long, 14″ deep, 20″ high, **$500.**

Another statement claimed that many competitors marketed go-carts that had no springs. They would jolt. They would jar. They could cause serious injuries, resulting in deformities. Steel, coiled springs in Sears' go-carts promoted smooth rides without harming the children. Of course, a no-spring go-cart could be shipped, but why not consider the infant's welfare and pay slightly more for a safer product?

People now jog or run for health and sport, but years ago strolling allowed them to be out in the fresh air. In small towns it was friendly to greet everyone you met, and frequently a walk was disrupted while people stopped to exchange news. If an indulgent mama and papa were out with their newborn tucked in a baby carriage, naturally the infant had to be inspected by neighboring veranda sitters and other strollers. The viewers had to utter the acceptable appreciation. "Pretty baby. Pretty baby. Kitchy, kitchy coo. Looks just like

Baby buggy with parasol top, 48″ long, 20″ deep, 62″ high. Natural reed. Circa late 1800s, **$525.**

Baby buggy, wire wheels, scrolls, serpentine or rollfront, 50½″ long, 20½″ deep, 35″ high. Circa late 1800s, **$495.**

you, Myrtle, but she has her papa's eyes, doesn't she, Oliver?"

Carriages for twins had a parasol at each end, and the babies were placed facing each other, tiny toes together. A brake came to be a safety feature by the 1900s. Some of the reed carriages had a feature that linked them to go-carts — adjustable back supports for sitting. When slipped down, these formed bed bases. By the late 1920s "baby buggy" had replaced "carriage."

Wooden rocking horse with wicker seat, 38″ long, 12″ wide, 20″ high, **$195.**

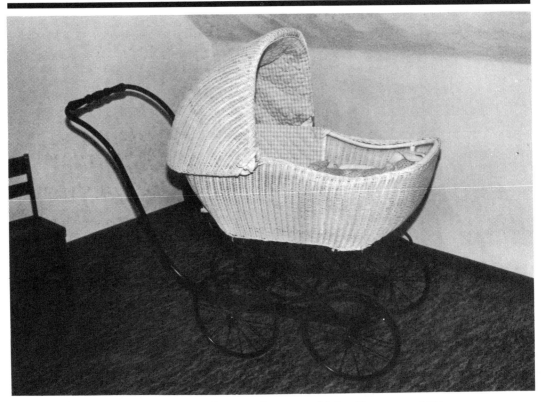

Baby buggy, rubber wheels, metal spokes, 43″ long, 42″ high. Circa 1920, **$175.**

Chairs similar to mama's and papa's were made in child sizes, and a whole family could rock together. Straight chairs, sofas, and lounges also came in petite sizes for the little people.

Doll settee, 13½″ arm to arm, 12″ high, **$150.** Cradle with gesso flowers, 8″ long, 5″ deep, 8″ high, **$85.**

Baby buggy, 44″ long, 17½″ deep, 43″ high. Circa 1930, **$150.**

Child's rocker with Armand Marseille doll, 18″ wide, 24″ high. Circa late 1800s, **$150.**

Child's rocker with decorative balls and scrolls, 18″ wide, 24½″ high. Circa late 1800s, **$140.**

Child's armchair rocker, rolled arms and seat, 18″ arm to arm, 28″ high. Circa 1920. Seat and back need repair, **$150.**

Child's rocker, 16″ arm to arm, 21″ high. Circa 1910, **$150.**

Child's rocker with slip cushion, 20″ arm to arm, 22″ high. Circa 1920, **$165.**

Child's chair with rolled arms, 24″ wide, 26½″ high. Circa 1910, **$165.**

Child's sofa, 41″ wide, 18″ deep, 24½″ high. Circa 1920, **$350.**

Child's lounge chair and footrest. Chair: 33″ wide, 18¼″ deep, 26″ high. Footrest: 17″ wide, 20″ deep, 11″ high. Circa 1920. **Set, $135.**

Child's rocker with cushion, 14½″ arm to arm, 24½″ high. Circa late 1920s, **$95.**

Doll highchair, cane seat, wicker braided back (needs repair); 7″ arm to arm, 22″ high, **$135.**

Child's rocker with pressed solid weave cane seat and wooden base, 14″ arm to arm, 24″ high. Circa 1920, **$215.**

Child's rocker, fiber weave, 20″ wide, 19″ high. Circa 1920, **$125.**

Doll swing with wardrobe beneath, sea grass; 6″ square, 19″ high, **$250.**

Two utilitarian chairs for toddlers met special needs. The highchair, or chair with table (tray), stood ready at mealtime. These chairs could be purchased with or without the tray, so if you see one missing this table section it may have been bought that way originally. A version referred to as a "nursery chair" in more modest days would be termed a potty chair today.

Child's highchair, 13½″ wide, 38″ high. Circa late 1800s, **$225.**

Child's highchair, 16½″ wide, 40″ high. Circa 1915, **$225.**

Child's highchair, 16¼″ arm to arm, 21″ deep, 32½″ high. Circa 1920, **$225.** Wastebasket, 12½″ diameter, 9″ high, **$30.**

Potty chair, 12″ wide, 10″ deep, 17½″ high. Circa early 1900s, **$125.**

Potty chair, 13″ wide, 10″ deep, 19″ high. Circa early 1900s. Needs repair, **$75.**

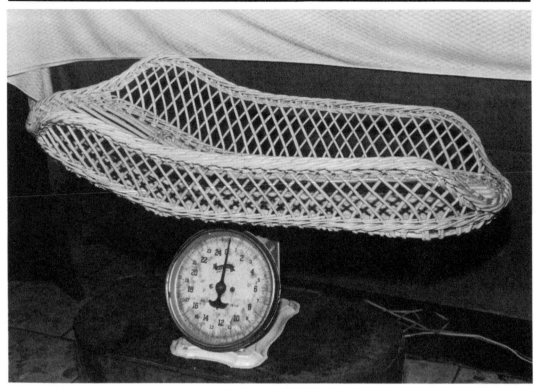

Baby basket on scale can be unscrewed to use as baby carrier, 28″ long, 13″ deep, 5″ high. Circa 1920, **$85.**

When the development of babies was charted by their weight, a wicker basket on top of the scale served as a safe depository for the infant while his or her poundage was noted. One with a dual purpose had a basket that could be unscrewed to form a carrier for transport.

When the little one grew old enough to play, wicker served again. Toys frequently are imitations of adult-sized articles. A variety of these miniatures were made especially for wee ones to enjoy, but doll carriages and cradles were special favorites when children wanted to "play house."

Doll cradle, 15″ long, 9″ wide, 16″ high. Circa 1920, **$110.**

Doll cradle, 17″ long, 9″ wide, 17½″ high. Circa 1920, **$95.**

Doll buggy, 29″ long, 8½″ wide, 24″ high. Circa 1915, **$225.**

Doll buggy, 29″ long, 9″ wide, 26″ high. Circa 1915, **$250.**

Nine-piece dollhouse furniture set; as a size example, the chaise longue is 6½″ long, 3″ deep at back, 3″ high. **Set: $350.**

Doll buggy, 29″ long, 9″ wide, 26½″ high. Circa 1920, **$250.**

Salesman's sample or prototype of a four-piece parlor set made by Lloyd Manufacturing Co.; settee, 11″ arm to arm, 7″ high; armchair, 7″ arm to arm, 7″ high; table, 6½″ diameter, 4½″ high. **Set: $400.**

In horse and buggy days a sulky was a light, two-wheeled carriage for a single occupant that was pulled by a horse. A passenger could be elite and aloof while riding in it. These small vehicles are doll-sized versions (right).

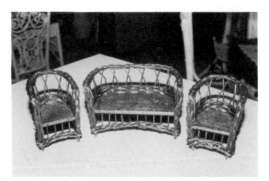

Three-piece doll parlor set, wooden seats, braided reed; settee, 9″ arm to arm, 5½″ high; chairs, 4½″ arm to arm, 6″ high. **Set: $125.**

Doll sulky, 36″ long. Circa 1915, **$250.**

Doll sulky, 45″ long. Circa 1915, **$225.**

Doll sulky, 50″ long, 19″ deep, 32″ high. Circa 1920, **$285.**

Doll buggy, 34″ long, 11½″ deep, 32″ high. Circa 1920, **$175.**

Label on doll sulky.

It is interesting that the word *sulky*, meaning sullen or withdrawn, is derived from the name of this one-person carriage.

Adults seize children's furniture and toys of yesteryear to collect. If they are ardent doll fans, their infants and fashionable ladies repose in life-like postures. In this manner, they utilize these nostalgic reminders of childhood. Because collectors are interested, wee wicker items from the 1800s and early 1900s are being preserved.

4 Sitting Pretty

During the last century, wicker invaded the porch, parlor, sun rooms, reception areas, resort verandas, club rooms, and hotels. It was made in child as well as in adult sizes. Porches appeared light and happy when wicker furniture invited guests to sit, chat, and relax.

Reed, cane, rattan, and willow enjoy being outdoors because "Raindrops Falling on My Head" could be their theme song. Since they are products of nature, water helps prevent them from drying out. To man-made fiber, however, water can be dangerous because the twisted paper treated with glue

sizing can be damaged by an excess of moisture. In spite of this, fiber has some advantages. It is relatively inexpensive and very flexible, while the "stick type" can be broken.

Indoor wicker provided comfort, plus class. Much of the handcrafted woven work was ornamental, creative in design, and bright in appearance. Some articles were given descriptive names. Victorian homes usually had large entrance halls, and hall or reception chairs served there. The version with the low back could fit an angle, so it was also termed a corner chair.

Corner chair with heart scrolls, 26" deep, 29" high, **$275**.

Entry way or photographer's chair, 20" wide, 42" high, **$425**.

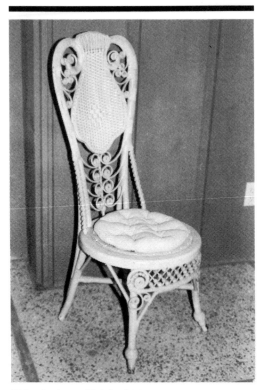

Side chair, 43″ high, **$325.**

Reception chair, 17½″ wide, 39″ high. Pressed
seat, brass caps on feet, **$250.**

Window seat, 34″ wide, 18″ deep, 29½″ high, **$350.**

At times various manufacturers assigned different titles to similar objects. A family could decide on a special use for some item, and that would be what they would call it. This small backless piece of furniture, therefore, is a fireside bench, vanity chair, or window seat. All these designations have something in common. The seat could be employed when its occupants desired to look at something special. It's fun to watch the lively flames in a fireplace. A woman needs a chair and a mirror when she combs her long locks. A seat placed before a window allows one to enjoy the view. Because of its versatility this bench has acquired many names, assigned according to its use. Would you believe that some distributors even dubbed it an exotic Turkish chair?

This tub chair with its rolled arms is made of German reed. It has a curtain or apron front under the seat that has a slight resemblance to a basket.

A lady's rocker with a pocket for magazines was small in size. If the owner sought to sew, her materials could be kept handy. Some refer to this as a nurse rocker since a mother could keep small objects near for baby or nurse the child while seated comfortably. The requirements of the user determine its moniker.

Tub chair, 25″ wide, 29″ high, **$350.**

Victorian anchor-back-design chair; 21″ arm to arm, 36″ high, **$325.**

Sewing rocker with pocket, 17½″ wide, 33½″ high; pocket is 5″ wide, **$265.**

Lift seat settee, 41" wide, 18" deep, 29" high, **$600.**

Settee, 41" wide, 20" deep, 39" high, **$325.**

The plain boxy style of furniture that is known as Mission was popular in the first two decades of the 1900s. It is exemplified by a small lift-top settee.

Other articles went straight after being influenced by Mission styles.

Since wicker chairs were light in weight, they were easy to set up in funeral parlor chapels. These small straight chairs earned the title "funeral parlor chairs." The owners of these bought them from such establishments.

Here is another way a name came to be attached to certain wicker pieces. It became increasingly expensive for furniture factories to import Far Eastern, French, German, or East Indian reed. And the hand labor required to craft tightly woven furniture and specialized patterns with their ornate scrolls proved costly. Around 1900,

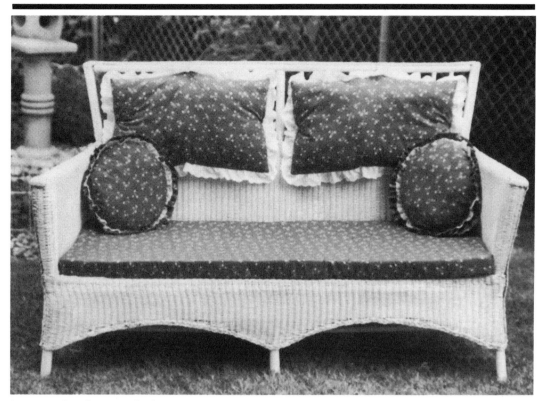

Settee, 53" wide, 31½" high, **$550.**

Funeral parlor chair, 36" high, **$150.**

Funeral parlor side chair, 37" high, **$95.**

Side chair with Art Deco design, woven in back, 37″ high, **$175.**

Armchair, 29″ arm to arm, 32″ high, **$235.**

companies seeking to cut expenses turned to open work designs, which took less material and required less work. Because these new wicker rockers populated fashionable resort verandas where the society set gathered, they were called "Bar Harbor" rockers.

Art Deco receives its Frenchy sound from an international exposition of modern art that was held in Paris in 1925. The proper title was "Exposition Internationale des Arts Decoratifs et Industriels Modernes." This promoted interest in cubism and geometric forms. The diamond design on the back of wicker in the late 1920s and the 1930s is attributed to the decorative style that emerged. Sometimes the pattern was colored to create added emphasis and to cause it to stand out from its background. Actually, these geometric designs were in vogue before the exposition, but they do fit the Art Deco concepts.

Rocker with upholstered back, wings and seat; 29″ arm to arm, 36″ high, **$495.** Floor lamp, 27″ diameter shade, 74″ high, **$650.** Collapsible butler's tray, turned wooden legs, lift-off wooden tray with wicker edging, 18″ wide, 13″ deep, 28″ high, **$125.**

Three-piece Bar Harbor set made by the Ypsilanti Reed Furniture Co., Ionia, Michigan. Armchair, 27″ arm to arm, 35″ high; rocker, 27″ arm to arm, 33″ high; sofa, 80″ long, 35″ high. **Set, $1,250.**

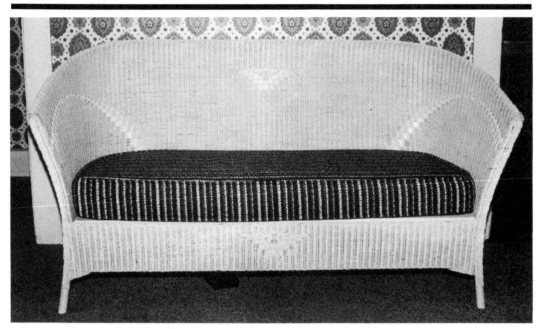

Settee, fiber made, 60″ arm to arm, 30″ high, **$625.**

Around 1929-1930 stick reed emerged. Removable spring cushions were generally upholstered with sturdy, bright, floral cretonne.

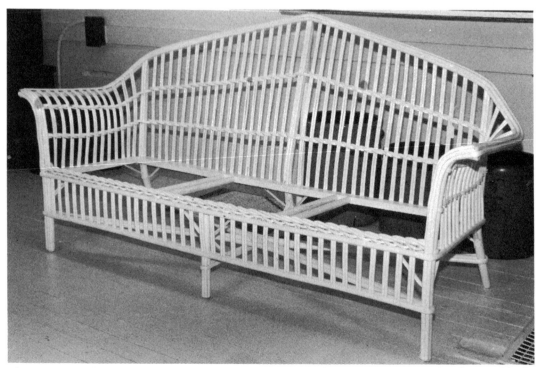

Three-piece stick reed set. Sofa with cushions removed to show construction, 69″ wide, 33½″ high; chairs, 28″ arm to arm, 32½″ high. **Set, $800.**

A label supplies information. If there is no identifying tag, the way to determine whether an old piece was hand done or machined is to examine the ends of the woven material. When the component parts are solid, it's natural, perhaps rattan, reed, cane, willow, or a combination. Material twisted in rope-like fashion with end strands that can be separated and seen as wrapped together are indicative of man-made twisted fiber. While various grasses also could be twisted together and tightly woven by hand, they usually present a more bumpy, slightly less even appearance. Not much furniture was fashioned completely in this manner. Grasses were employed more frequently to add decorative ball feet or panels or other small ornamental touches rather than to form whole articles of furniture.

Rocker with Lloyd loom tight weave, 27" arm to arm, 32" high, **$225.**

Label on rocker.

Settee, reed construction with pressed seat, 38½″ wide, 17½″ deep, 38″ high, **$625.**

In the picture of the settee (left above) notice that the hand-woven tight weave is slightly bulkier than the Lloyd-loomed sofa (below) and the lines are not as precise and soldier straight. Style provides an added bonus. Ornate weaves announce vainly, "Look at me. I'm an original. I'm hand fashioned." A manufacturer's label, the material used, the precision of the weave, and the style unite to differentiate the hand woven from the machine loomed.

Photographer's chair with Simon & Halbig doll, 34″ wide, 43″ high, **$600.**

Sofa with Lloyd loom tight weave, 72″ wide, 33″ high, **$500.**

Victorian wicker furniture tended to be a singles operation — a lone chair, a separate table, a settee in its own design. Apparently, in the early 1900s, the Noah's Ark concept of two-by-two mates who should go forth and be fruitful and multiply predominated. Complete sets became the norm. A housewife could select a sofa, a rocking chair or two, a couple of armchairs, and a table that were alike. Wasn't it delightful? Her whole room matched! Perhaps when creativity of design disappeared, women tired of the sameness, and the desire to have wicker furniture declined temporarily.

Wide bottom, handmade divan. Circa 1901. 34" wide, 18" deep, 38" high, **$565.**

Settee, 35" wide, 31" high, **$400.**

Three-piece set. Sofa, 70″ wide, 31″ high; rocker, 30″ wide, 29″ high; chair, 30″ wide, 30″ high. **Set, $800.**

Three-piece set. Rocker, 27½″ arm to arm, 30″ high; armchair, 27″ arm to arm, 34½″ high; oval table, 24″ by 36″ top, 29½″ high. **Set, $750.**

Three-piece tight fiber weave set. Rocker, 26″ arm to arm, 38″ high; sofa, 65″ wide, 37½″ high; chair, 25″ arm to arm, 38″ high. **Set, $1,200.**

Settee with pressed cane seat, 48″ wide, 31″ high, **$800.**

Sofa, 73½″ wide, 34″ high, **$450.**

Settee, 50″ wide, 20″ deep, 40″ high, **$425.**

Settee without arms, machine woven, 37″ wide, 31″ high, **$350.**

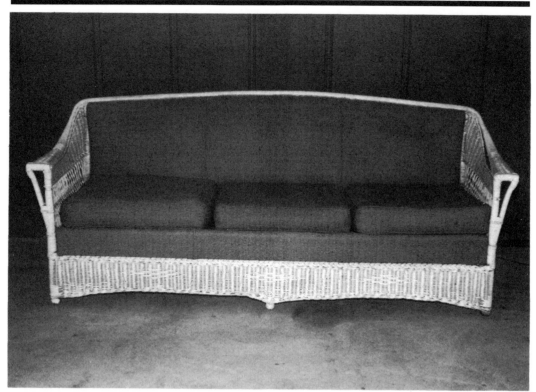

Sofa, upholstered seat and back with heavy metal springs, 84″ wide, 34″ high, **$550.**

Sofa, 64″ wide, 21″ deep, 35″ high. Circa 1960s, **$525.**

Sofa, 76″ wide, 24″ deep, 31″ high, **$250.**

Settee, 57″ arm to arm, 33″ high. Circa 1950s, **$350.**

Armchair with cane seat, 22″ arm to arm, 35″ high, **$260.**

Side chair, 20″ wide, 42½″ high, **$250.**

Round back side chair, 29″ wide, 32″ high, **$450.**

Two-piece Heywood-Wakefield set, Roll back chair, 33″ arm to arm, 33″ high; roll back rocker, 34″ arm to arm, 31″ high. Each piece, **$500.**

Heywood-Wakefield label from two-piece set.

Side chair with cutout "peek-a-boo" was a prevalent style in 1915, 16½″ wide, 34½″ high, **$175.**

Armchair, 24″ arm to arm, 37″ high, **$240.**

Armchair with six legs and woven cane seat, 23″ arm to arm, 33½″ high, **$375.**

Armchair with rolled arms, 27″ arm to arm, 34″ high, **$350.**

Lounge chair frame, 24″ arm to arm, 34″ high. Upholstered section was being upholstered. **Frame only, $155.**

Desk or side chair, 36″ high, **$175.**

Armchair, 29″ arm to arm, 32½″ high, **$240.**

Armchair, 31″ arm to arm, 36″ high, **$245.**

Armchair with extension for "coffee break" on right and magazine holder on left, 34″ wide, 32½″ high, **$375.**

Armchair, 32″ wide, 35″ high, **$350.**

Armchair with two lidded magazine holders, 33″ arm to arm, 40″ high, **$400.**

Armchair with label that reads "Karpen Guaranteed Construction Furniture, Chicago, Michigan City, N.Y." Art Deco design. 34″ arm to arm, 36″ high, **$240.**

Armchair, 22″ wide, 31″ high, **$350.**

Armchair, 30″ arm to arm, 30″ high, **$225.**

Armchair, 30″ arm to arm, 30″ high, **$225.**

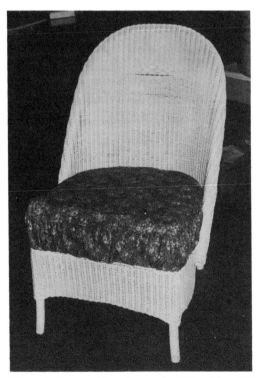

Side chair, machine loomed, 20″ wide, 32″ high, **$200.**

Armchair, 32″ arm to arm, 33″ high, **$165.**

A square plant stand, **$150**, and an oval table with a wooden top, **$325**, provide resting places for the greenery in this upstairs room.

Entry hall is given color and interest with a birdcage, **$310**, and a settee, **$350**.

Kitchen area with wall decorations, including wicker rug beater, **$45**, and fireside or Turkish chair with doll, **$310**.

Victorian wicker scene with a round table, **$425**; sweetheart rocker, **$425**; and music stand, **$395**.

Kitchen area featuring a highchair, **$275**; buffet, **$850**; natural reed flower basket, **$125**; and doll's highchair, **$125**.

In the bedroom a chaise longue, **$625**, waits for a tired traveler.

Den area showing an urn-type basket, **$75**; a Victorian recamier, **$1,000**; and a Victorian sewing stand, **$385**.

Living room set with a basket for plants, **$75**; a settee, **$625**; corner table, **$350**; and table lamp, **$275**.

The corner of this blue bedroom is furnished with a side chair, **$155**, a rectangular table, **$210**, and a sewing rocker, **$165.**

Casual corner shows a rocking chair, **$350**, and a three-tier muffin stand, **$250.**

Living room area with sewing rocker, **$275**, round table, **$175**, three-cushioned sofa, **$350**, and basket on table, **$45**.

Fireplace setting showing two matching armchairs, **$250** each, and a sofa, **$475**.

The Wanna Buy a Duck shop in Canton, Ohio, specializes in wicker furniture. According to proprietor Carroll Swope, footstools and ottomans are difficult to find. Perhaps because of their elusive ways, they sell well. Vic and Anne Durkin of The Antique Repair Shop in Hammond, Indiana, made a similar statement when interviewed. They, too, are wicker advocates.

Footstool, 16″ diameter, 23″ high, **$200.**

Footstool with cushion, 14½″ wide, 12″ deep, 8″ high, **$125.**

Footstool, 16″ wide, 11″ deep, 21″ high, **$150.**   Footstool, 19½″ square, 17″ high, **$175.**

Footstool, 20″ wide, 12″ deep, 12½″ high, **$155.**

Footstool, 20″ wide, 13″ deep, 16″ high, **$275.**

Apparently people in the late Victorian Era liked patented furniture that did something unusual. For example, there were beds that folded up in the daytime to form desks. Children's highchairs could be pushed down to convert into strollers or rocking chairs. Rockers that rode on upside-down rungs or jolted on springs were found in wicker and are referred to in old catalogs as "patent rockers." The daintier version was for the lady of the house, the one with more generous proportions was for the gentleman. Today they are generally called platform rockers because they are constructed with a base.

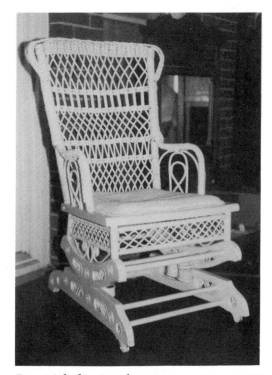

Patent (platform) rocker, 20″ arm to arm, 27″ deep, 36″ high, **$550.**

Patent (platform) rocker, 26″ arm to arm, 43″ high, **$385.**

Patent (platform) rocker, pressed cane seat, 20″ wide, 16″ deep, 35″ high, **$525.**

Fanback rocker, 25″ arm to arm, 38½″ high, **$375.**

Rocker, 18¼″ wide, 16″ deep, 39″ high, **$425.**

Rocker, rolled arm, cane in back, 23½" arm to arm, 37" high, **$375.**

Rocker, 24" arm to arm, 39" high, **$550.**

Rocker, pressed cane seat missing, 24" wide, 40" high, **$450.**

Rocker, 23" arm to arm, 37" high, **$425.**

Rocker, 25″ arm to arm, 37½″ high, **$650.**

Rocker, 35″ high, **$375.**

Rocker with wicker decorations in wooden frame, 24″ arm to arm, 39″ high, **$275.**

Rocker, 25″ arm to arm, 36″ high, **$325.**

Rocker, pressed cane seat, demi arms, 38″ high, **$285.**

Rocker, serpentine or rolled arms and back, 27″ arm to arm, 42″ high, **$350.**

Rocker, 28½″ arm to arm, 41″ high, **$295.**

Rocker, 25¼″ arm to arm, 44½″ high, **$210.**

Rocker, 36" high. Needs repair, **$245.**

Rocker, pressed cane seat, 26" arm to arm, 47" high, **$435.**

Rocker, slip-cushion seat, fiber, 31" arm to arm, 36" high, **$260.**

Rocker, circa 1920, 32" arm to arm, 33" high, **$175.**

Rocker, replaced rockers, slip cushion, 31″ arm to arm, 30″ high, **$265.**

Rocker, fiber, slip cushion, Art Deco design in back, 30″ arm to arm, 36″ high, **$255.**

Rocker, willow and rattan, slip cushion seat, 28″ arm to arm, 37½″ high, **$345.**

Rocker, 33″ arm to arm, 31″ high, **$125.**

Rocker, fiber, demi arms, slip cushion, 17" wide, 31" high, **$155.**

Rocker, 23" wide, 29" high, **$325.**

Rocker, 26" arm to arm, 37" high, **$245.**

Rocker with magazine basket, 29" arm to arm, 32" high, **$325.**

Prior to air conditioning days, porches served as the summer social center. Young people enjoyed gathering there of an evening to swing and sway. If someone could play the "uke" (ukelele) or banjo, impromptu sing-alongs might result. The swings were gentle, not the type enjoyed by children. Wouldn't you enjoy a wicker swing? You would be sitting pretty!

Rocker, 29″ arm to arm, 30″ high, **$295.**

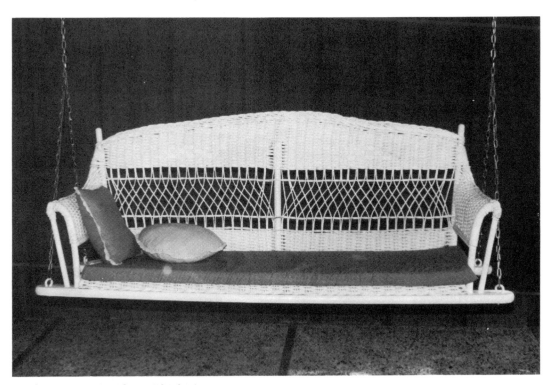

Porch swing, 72″ wide, 24″ high, **$425.**

Porch swing, 54″ wide, 20″ deep, 18″ high, **$525.**

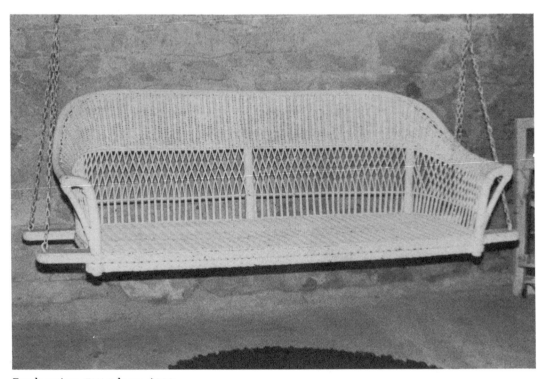

Porch swing, 74½″ long, **$800.**

Tables come in all shapes and sizes and frequently receive their names from the purpose they fulfill. To illustrate this point, here is an extravagant late Victorian example. It probably served as a lamp table, judging from the fact that its rectangular top is not very large. The round table has what people currently term "elephant trunk legs." Its bulb feet are woven from sea grass. The square "elephant" table has a base shelf with a fine, close weave usually found in the use of sea grasses. Both tables dwarf the scrolled, rattan-wrapped lamp table with its cane insert in the top.

End table, woven cane in wooden frame for top, 18″ square, 30″ high, **$155.**

Round table with wooden insert top, 30″ diameter, 30″ high, **$425.**

Square table with bottom shelf, 24″ square, 29¼″ high, **$400.**

Usually, the ardent wicker collector likes the tops of tables and desks to be of a woven material rather than of oak or some other hard wood. Here are tables that have this characteristic.

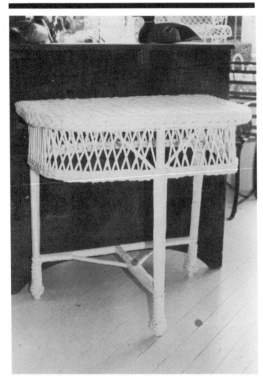

Parlor table, 31″ wide, 21″ deep, 30″ high, **$260.**

Round table, 24″ diameter, 27″ high, **$250.**

Round table, braided edge base shelf, 30½″ diameter, 28½″ high, **$250.**

Round table with shelf, 27½″ diameter, 30¼″ high, **$120.**

Round lamp table, 21″ diameter, 26½″ high, **$160.**

Oval parlor table, 28″ wide, 19″ deep, 25″ high, **$250.**

Rectangular table with magazine shelf, 22″ wide, 15″ deep, 24″ high, **$145.**

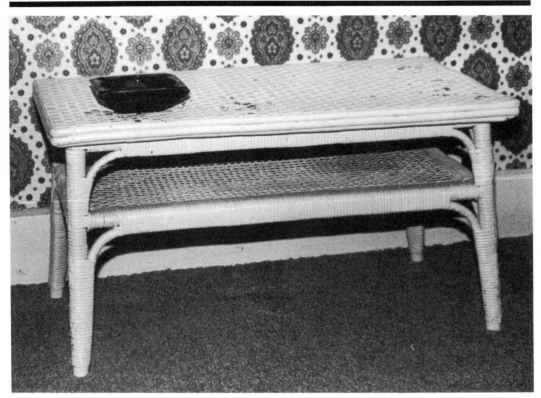

Coffee table, 30½" wide, 16½" deep, 16" high. Late 1940s, **$85.**

Tables with wooden tops have interesting features to offer.

Oval parlor table, 38" wide, 25½" deep, 30" high, **$275.**

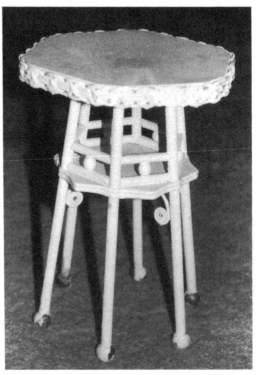

Plant stand, six sided, 12" wide, 18" high, **$95.**

Oval parlor table, 36″ wide, 24″ deep, 30″ high, **$300.**

Rectangular parlor table, 32″ wide, 18″ deep, 29″ high, **$250.**

Oval parlor table, 45½″ wide, 26″ deep, 30″ high, **$275.**

Round, two-tiered table, 30″ diameter, 29½″ high, **$295.**

Oval table with two magazine racks, 30″ wide, 20½″ deep, 30″ high, **$250.**

Oval table, Heywood-Wakefield, Chicago, Illinois, 29½″ wide, 20½″ deep, 30″ high, **$250.**

Rectangular parlor table with walled shelf at base, 28″ wide, 19″ deep, 29″ high, **$210.** Table lamp, 26″ high, **$130.**

Oval table with wooden inset top, 36½" wide, 20½" deep, 30" high, **$250.**

Oval table with magazine rack at base, 29" wide, 13" deep, 25" high, **$250.**

Library table with bottom shelf, 42" wide, 26" deep, 30" high, **$300.**

Oval table, 34″ wide, 18″ deep, 28½″ high, **$250.**

Oval table, 41½″ wide, 19½″ deep, 30½″ high, **$250.**

Oval library table with label that reads "Karpen Guaranteed Construction Furniture, Chicago, Michigan City, New York." 46" wide, 18" deep, 30" high, **$315.**

Oval table with chestnut top and magazine holders at inside of each end, 49" wide, 21" deep, 30" high, **$295.** Table lamp, 21" diameter, 24" high; 5" silk fringe on shade, **$275.**

Round table with wooden top and base shelf, 27" diameter, 30" high, **$375.**

Although Thomas A. Edison invented the incandescent bulb to produce electric light in 1879, it took years before power lines spread to all cities. Electricity did not reach many rural areas until the 1930s or later and before then there was no need for lamps made of wicker. Such woven material was combustible and unsuitable for use with kerosene or gas flames. Thus wicker lamps generally date to this century.

The bases of some floor lamps have been compared to the shape of the Eiffel Tower in Paris and they take their name from this resemblance.

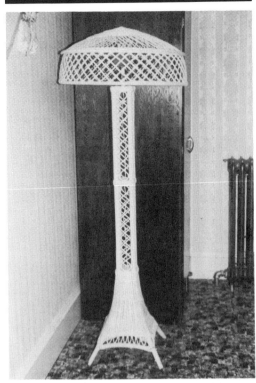

Floor lamp, 69″ high; shade diameter, 27″, **$675.**

Floor lamp, 62″ high; shade diameter, 26″, **$750.**

Eiffel Tower floor lamp, 28″ diameter shade, 72″ high, **$875.**

Floor lamp with metal ballerina design on shade support, 19″ diameter shade, 66″ high, **$475.** Art Deco design desk chair, 36″ high, **$135.**

When a shade has fringe dangling from it, it reminds people of the unconventional, vibrant girls of the 1920s who wore both their hair and their dresses considerably shorter than their mothers did. They were called flappers, and the fringe decorations on their dresses swished about as they danced the Charleston. Because of this the shades are considered to be of flapper age.

Floor lamp, 58″ high; shade diameter, 12″, **$500.**

Floor lamp, 68" high; shade diameter, 26", **$600.**

Table lamps were also needed in homes serviced by the new electrical power.

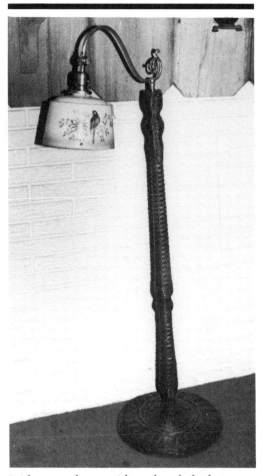

Bridge type lamp with replaced shade, 46½" high, **$225.**

Table lamp, 25" high, **$200.**

Remember while you are enjoying all your wicker pieces that similar types existed for a time. Rolled armchair styles introduced in the late 1800s were still around in the early 1900s. If you want to be safe, put "circa" or "c" before your dates. That allows for a range of years on either side of the date you list.

Table lamp, 26″ high, **$275.**

Table lamp, 22″ high, **$155.**

Table lamp, 14″ high, **$85.**

Table lamp, 23″ high; shade diameter, 20″, **$220**. Footstool, 18″ diameter, **$220**.

Table lamp, 24″ high; shade diameter, 19½″, **$225**. Round table, 26″ diameter, 26″ high, **$250**.

Rocker, 29″ arm to arm, 34″ high, **$210**.

Desk, 28½″ wide, 18″ deep, 30″ high, **$300**. Table lamp with pull chain and weighted base, 10″ diameter shade, 16″ high, **$195**. Bench with lift-lid storage unit, 34″ arm to arm, 12″ deep, 25″ high, **$275**.

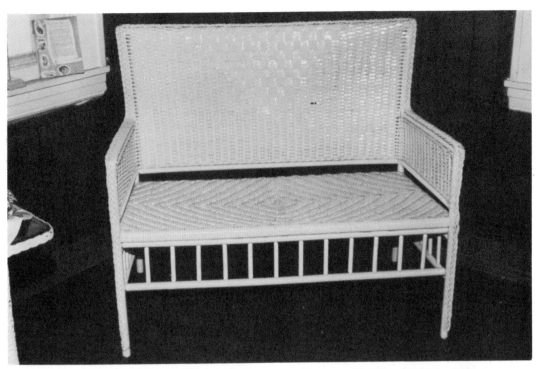

Settee or love seat with diamond herringbone pattern in seat; 43″ wide, 36″ high, **$450.**

Chaise longue with one arm shorter for easier accessibility; 35″ arm to arm, 58″ long, 36″ high, **$895.**

Gate-leg table, 44″ diameter, 29½″ high, with 13½″ drop leaves, **$1,200.**

Rocker, 28″ arm to arm, 38″ high, **$245.**

Victorian platform rocker, 27″ arm to arm, 43″ high, **$600.**

White Victorian rocker, 20″ arm to arm, 38″ high, **$325.** Natural reed rocker, 20″ arm to arm, 37″ high, **$425.**

Heywood Wakefield natural reed chair, 28″ arm to arm, 33″ high, **$575.**

Victorian love seat, 50″ arm to arm, 40″ high, **$850.**

Pair of chairs with club feet, 35″ high, **$245 each.**

Heywood Morriel slipper chair with knitted reed back, 34″ high, **$450.**

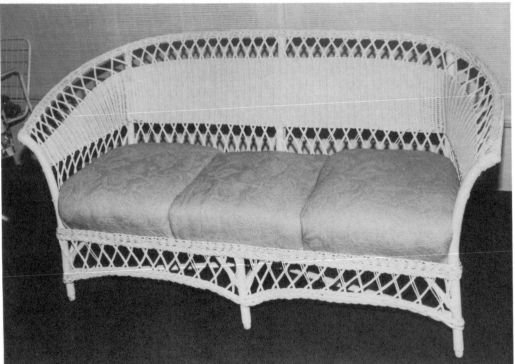

Three-piece fiber parlor set: sofa, 62″ arm to arm, 32″ high; chair, 30″ arm to arm, 32″ high; rocker, 29″ arm to arm, 31″ high. **Set: $1,200.** Fern stand, sea grass and reed, 11″ diameter, 27″ high, **$80.**

5 Wicker Work Items

Students need space for their study materials and a writing surface. Wicker desks were produced to meet these requirements, and they were available in hand woven patterns, tightly machine-made fiber, or in the open look. This Bar Harbor idea of the early 1900s saved labor costs and reduced the amount of material necessary. A light, airy appearance resulted.

Desk, 29″ wide, 17″ deep, 37″ high. Chair, 36″ high. **Set, $450.**

Kidney-shaped desk with ash top, 37″ wide, 22″ deep, 34″ high. Chair, 36″ high. **Set, $465.**

Kidney-shaped desk, with letter holders, 36″ wide, 19″ deep, 29¼″ high; rail 5″ high, **$350.**

Desk, 66¼" wide, 23" deep, 29" high, **$550.** Chair, 32" high, **$200.**

Desk, oak top and drawer front, 30½" wide, 20½" deep, 30½" high; rail 8½" high, **$350.**

Kidney-shaped desk, wooden top and wooden drawer front, 35" wide, 21" deep, 36" high, **$350.**

Magazine holder, 18″ wide, 14¼″ deep, 24½″ high, **$110.**

Bookcases and magazine racks could hold reference supplies or be utilized for recreational reading materials.

Bookcase, 19½″ wide, 14″ deep, 42″high, **$350.**

Heywood Wakefield natural reed workbasket; 17″ wide, 12″ deep, 36″ high including handle, **$195.**

Bookcase, 17½″ wide, 12½″ deep, 36″ high, **$325.**

Magazine holder, 15″ wide, 5″ deep, 18½″ high, **$150.**

Magazine basket, 14″ wide, 9½″ high, **$45.**

Someone wondered why wicker music racks from the late 1800s and early 1900s seem to be so prevalent today. Those were the days before radio and television brought popular tunes or the classics into the home. Pittsburgh radio station KDKA broadcast the results of the 1920 presidential election, which declared Warren Harding the winner. This was a first, and the 1920s marked an extension of the programs developed to please and inform the public. But before the media expanded, people created their own music. If there was a parlor organ or piano, families and guests sang around it. Sheet music or songbooks with favorite hymns could be kept on a stand. If someone in the family were taking lessons, space was required for the instructional material. This helps explain why music racks were so popular.

Music stand, 19″ wide, 15½″ deep, 47″ high, **$375.**

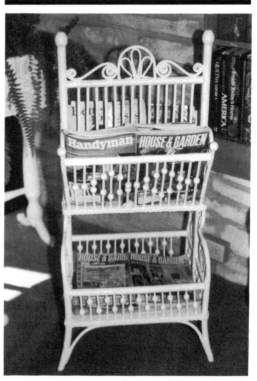

Music stand, 17″ wide, 14″ deep, 38″ high, **$385.**

Woven clothes hampers, then as now, served as receptacles for dirty clothes for the whole family. What some old catalogs termed "work baskets" are usually designated sewing hampers now.

Clothes hamper, 23″ wide, 14″ deep, 26″ high, **$70.**

Clothes hamper, 22″ wide, 17½″ deep, 25½″ high, **$65.**

Clothes hamper, 16½″ wide, 8″ deep, 21″ high, **$65.**

Sewing basket, 21″ wide, 17″ deep, 36″ high, **$350.**

Sewing basket, 16″ wide, 12″ deep, 27″ high, **$235.**

Planter or dry sink, 27″ wide, 20″ deep, 29″ high at front, 33″ high at back, **$235.**

The use for this small stand is perplexing and the all encompassing term *work basket* may be sufficient. At any rate, its ingenious owner has put it to work holding a supply of towels in the bathroom.

Corner clothes hamper, 22″ wide, 16″ deep, 27″ high, **$65.**

Lift top stand (used for towels), 14″ wide, 12″ deep, 25″ high, **$100.**

Buttocks basket, 19½" wide, 14" deep, 11" high. Circa 1860-1870, **$90.**

Because people needed to carry things such as nuts, eggs, fruits, vegetables, and herbs, they fashioned baskets and utensils long before they created woven furniture. The twig construction of this buttocks basket can be seen clearly. A collector dates it to around 1860-1870. To put it crudely, the name comes from its resemblance to a human bum. It is pictured in the middle of the three baskets in the group below. It is turned upside down so the bottom and the twisted willow construction show.

From left to right: Round basket with handle, circa 1900, 17½" wide, 14½" deep, 16" high, **$75.** Buttocks basket, **$90.** Hanging half basket, 16" wide, 14" deep, 16" high, **$95.**

From left to right: Round basket with two handles, 11″ diameter, 7″ high, **$35.** Basket with twisted handle and wooden bottom, 16″ wide, 12″ deep, 15″ high, **$45.** Basket with wrapped handle, 14″ wide, 9½″ deep, 10½″ high, **$35.**

Lift lid basket, 31″ wide, 19″ deep, 18″ high, **$150.**

Clothes basket, 27″ wide, 22″ deep, 15″ high, **$55.**

Fishing creel. **$100.**

Splint basket, 26″ diameter, 18″ high, **$155.**

Wicker invalid chairs were advertised in the *Ladies' Home Journal* of March, 1899. It was said that some had fifty changes of positions. Those were referred to as reclining rolling chairs. When only one position was available, it was termed fixed. The one pictured has only a single position, could be self-propelled or pushed, and was made by the Chicago Wheel Co.

Invalid chair, self-propelled, 27″ wide, 44″ high, **$500.**

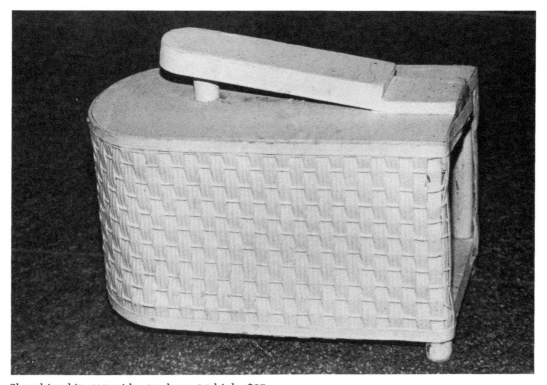

Shoeshine kit, 11″ wide, 6″ deep, 9″ high, **$65.**

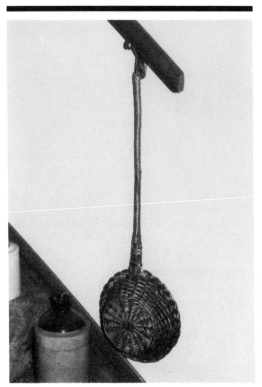

Church collection basket, 27″ long, 9″ diameter, **$145.**

This long-handled basket had a noble work record. A deacon or usher in a church passed it among the worshipers to receive their offerings.

Storage cabinet or server with lift top, 22″ wide, 13″ deep, 29″ high, **$325.**

6 A Wicker Picker's Accessories

Ferneries filled with delicate sprawling greens or the bright glow of deep red geraniums add a cheerful touch to a wicker decorator's rooms. Not enough were seen in southern coastal malls or New England shops to allow for comparison shopping, but dealers in Iowa, Illinois, Indiana, and Ohio react to planters in a similar manner. "There are too many of them around," they moan. "You can't get much for a fernery." While an ornate style merits a higher price, common planters sell for under $100.

This seems odd at a time when plant stores abound, and homes appear to be wearing the green almost in St. Patrick's Day fashion. There should be a demand for planters.

What makes some ferneries distinctive? One pictured is unusually deep, and the back is higher than the front. The other has a different base with two legs that terminate in broad feet. The planting area itself is ovoid rather than rectangular. Because of these features, both planters earn a higher price tag.

Plant stand with back higher than front, 25½" wide, 18½" deep, 32" high, **$120.**

Plant stand, 32" wide, 11½" deep, 30½" high, **$165.**

Plant stand, 28" wide, 11" deep, 28" high, **$135.**

The next two are above average because the front bottom line is enhanced by a woven loop design. Dealers state that true collectors want their wicker natural, and the one below wears no white paint on its pristine surface. When a fernery has a feature that sets it apart, the cost increases. However, condition merits consideration. It must be competent to fill its mission, and it must be put in a good appearance.

Plant stand, 30" wide, 12" deep, 32" high, **$140.**

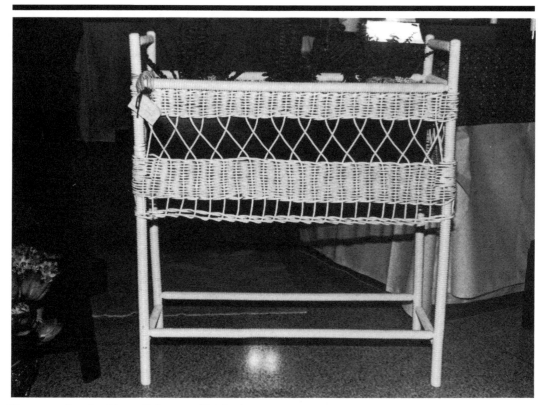

Plant stand, 28″ wide, 11″ deep, 31″ high, **$115.**

Plant stand, 29″ wide, 12″ deep, 30″ high, **$135.**

Plant stand, 27″ wide, 10½″ deep, 31″ high, **$110.**

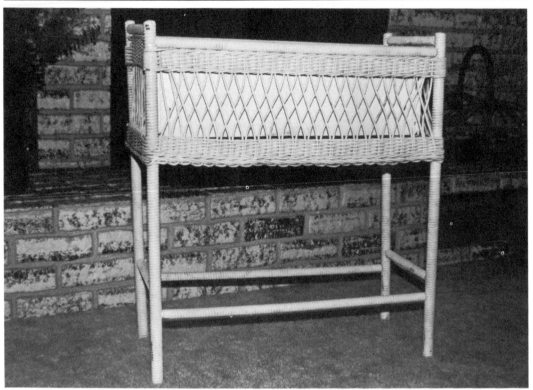

Plant stand, 27″ wide, 11″ deep, 30″ high, **$135.**

Plant stand, 12″ square, 30″ high, **$150.**

Plant stand, 11½″ square, 28″ high, **$120.**

Ferneries combined with birdcages brought nature indoors in the early decades of the 1900s. This one has the Bar Harbor open weave appearance.

The natural appearance of wicker combines well with growing greens whether they hang around the house, sit on something, or stand on the floor.

Plant stand with birdcage, 29" wide, 10" deep, 63" high, **$550.**

Hanging basket, 30" high, **$35.**

Plant basket, 15½" wide, 14½" deep, 15" high, **$50.**

Square planters with liners, 7½″ square, 5″ high, **$35 each.**

Plant stands are available in all shapes, sizes, and in a wide variety of designs.

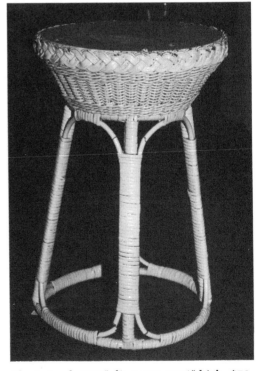

Plant stand, 10½″ diameter, 16½″ high, **$70.**

Plant stand, 12″ square, 26½″ high, **$70.**

Plant stand, 14½″ diameter, 36″ high, **$110.**

Plant stand, 11½″ diameter, 23½″ high, **$65.**

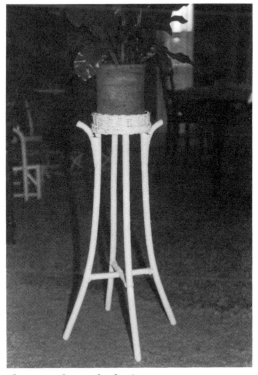

Plant stand, 28″ high, **$75.**

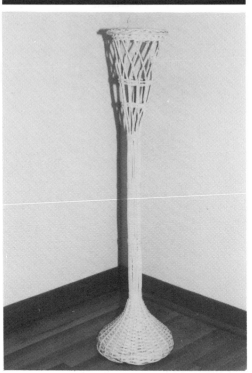

Plant stand, 7″ diameter, 36″ high, **$90.**

Plant stand, 16″ diameter, 31½″ high, **$200.**

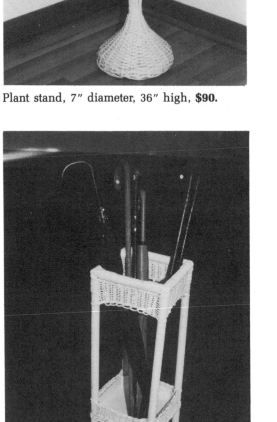

Umbrella stand, 10½″ square, 31″ high, **$165.**

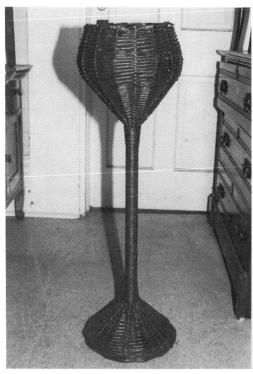

Plant stand, 8½″ diameter, 35½″ high, **$85.**

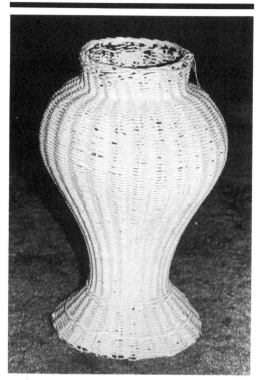

Basket urn, 7″ diameter at top, 19″ high, **$75.**

Birdcage stand, 74″ high, **$175.**

Both the bird and its house have flitted away from this holder, which serves now as an attractive planter.

"Tea carts sell well, if you can find them," dealers in various states say. While ferneries are in abundance, most of the tea carts must have rolled into exile in Hernando's Hideaway. Shop owners say they can't keep tea carts in stock.

Tea cart, 36″ long, 21″ deep, 30″ high, **$525.**

Tea cart, 38″ long, 23″ deep, 28″ high, **$525.**

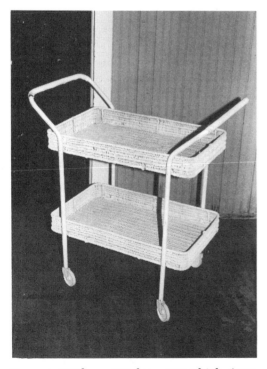

Tea cart, 36″ long, 26″ deep, 32½″ high, **$150.**

Tea cart, 35″ long, 18″ deep, 29″ high, **$450.**

Tea cart, original paint, 35″ long, 16″ deep, 34½″ high, **$550.**

Homes express the personality of their owners through the variety of ways they are decorated with wicker. These tea caddies are conversational pieces for two families who enjoy decorating in a distinct manner.

A tea server was a utilitarian and gracious piece for the dining room.

Tea server, 29″ wide, 16½″ deep, 28″ high, **$325.**

Lemonade caddy, 18″ diameter, 22″ high, **$125.**

Lemonade caddy, **$75.**

Tray and two candlesticks (console set), **$150.**

Even if you don't want wicker everywhere, you can be a wicker picker and accessorize with selected, unusual articles.

Desk organizer, 14″ wide, 8″ deep, 5½″ high, **$65.**

Fireplace screen, 29″ wide, 31½″ high, **$225.**

Mirror frame, 24½″ wide, 29½″ high, **$250.**

Oval frame, 10½″ by 7″, **$125.**

Hanging or floor shelf, 19″ wide, 15½″ deep, 25″ high, **$55.**

Purse with knobs for clasps, 13″ by 13″, **$42.**

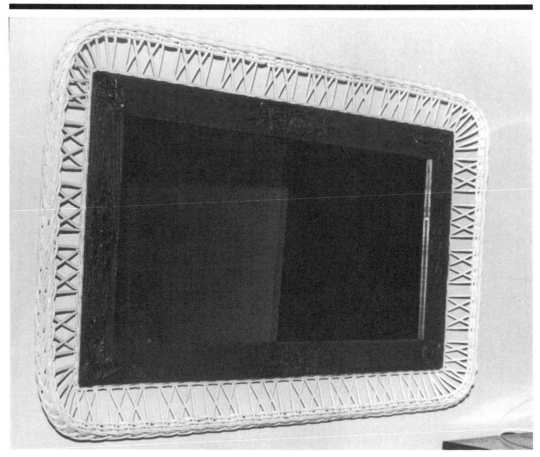

Oak frame with wicker border, 39½" wide, 25½" high, **$250.**

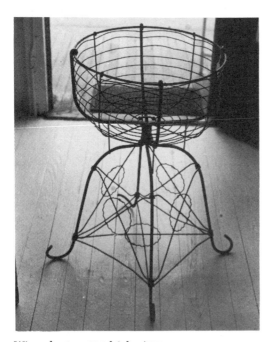

Wire planter, 36" high, **$95.**

Wanna Buy a Duck (the Swopes, 805 McKinley Ave. N.W., Canton, Ohio) suggested an idea for accessory items that complement wicker, which is their specialty.

"Wire and wicker are compatible," Carroll remarked.

Here are some attractive articles that have appeal and could keep company with wicker. According to Carroll, a wire planter goes well with herbs or moss and flowers growing in it.

Dainty benches such as these enhance wicker settings. While these are plain, some have fancy designs such as hearts.

Can't you visualize this delicate look as a go-along with wicker? Similar semicircular flower stands, available with or

Wire bench, 38″ wide, 38″ high, **$275.**

without a trellis, would hold one and one half to two dozen pots of beautiful foliage or blooming flowers, according to an 1897 advertisement.

Wire pieces could be adopted easily by wicker pickers.

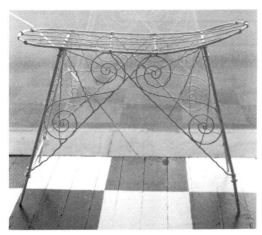

Wire bench, 23″ wide, 18″ high, **$65.**

Wire plant stand, 62″ high, **$275.**

7 I'll Take Mine Rare, Please

Did you know that Sarah Josepha Hale, who as editor of the magazine *Godey's Lady's Book* influenced thousands of women in the 1800s, played an indirect role in the making of the first phonograph in 1877?

When inventor Thomas Alva Edison sketched a simple mechanical cylinder and asked his shop foreman to make it, the surprised foreman complied, although he could not understand Edison's interest in something that was not chemical or electrical.

When he gave the completed project to his boss, curiosity caused the man to ask what it was, and Edison replied that the machine was going to talk. After putting tinfoil over the cylinder, he recited into the mouthpiece: "Mary Had a Little Lamb." Both he and his foreman were surprised when the contraption repeated the childish poem, one Widow Hale composed for her children. Of all his more than 1,100 inventions, the phonograph was Edison's favorite, and Mrs. Hale was probably pleased that he tested it with her poem.

Many other people also have found it enjoyable, including a woman who recently purchased a rare 1919-1920 model.

Did you read about the wicker floor model phonograph that was sold at an Iowa auction? The top bid was $1,400! This was brought up frequently when the prices of wicker items were discussed with dealers. Not too many people have seen a wicker cabinet made to house a record player of yore, including the authors of this book. One dealer did say she had a table type, but its lines were camouflaged amid a stack of wicker to be repaired in her garage.

The Antique Repair Shop owners in Hammond suggested shops to visit in Indiana, but the summer tourist traffic had reduced their inventory in wicker furniture. When one shop granted permission to take photographs, the proprietor exclaimed, "Oh, I have something stored in another location. I know you'll want to take its picture."

Facetiously, Bob replied, "And I know what it is — a wicker phonograph!"

The owner answered, "Yes, and it's a Heywood-Wakefield!"

Bob was amazed. He did not believe it was possible. As we followed the dealer's truck to the other site, a traffic light changed. She got through, but we were stuck as car after car separated us from the dealer — and in the excitement we had forgotten to ask her name. Fortunately, she stopped and waited for us. Soon, what to our wondering eyes should appear but a cane and reed phonograph with a brass tag at the rear inscribed "Heywood-Wakefield." And, the object of our attention was in mint condition!

The owner added yet another bit to the tale. The instrument did not work when she acquired it. Before she unloaded her prized purchase, she stopped at a shop where a man she knew repaired phonographs and had a personal collection of about fifty. Through the years he had sold "truckloads of them." When he saw the wicker wonder, he gazed in awe.

"In all my years of working with phonographs, I never saw a wicker cabinet before!" he exclaimed.

The dealer smiled joyously. "That's exactly what I wanted to hear!" she responded.

Examination showed that all the parts were intact. Excessive dirt and oil had gummed up the works, but all that was necessary was a good cleaning and this rare piece soon was tinkling out tunes again.

The instrument sold at the Iowa auction for $1,400 was listed as a "Luxfibre Phonograph (Wicker cabinet, phono needs minor

Heywood-Wakefield phonograph, three views, 18″ wide, 21″ deep, 43″ high, **$1,850.**

Cradle suspended in frame with round dome at top for mosquito netting, 37" long, 21" deep, 45" to dome top, **$575.**

Baby carrier, 17" wide, 9" deep, 32" high, **$385.**

repair)." The term "Luxfibre" suggests man-made fiber rather than natural materials. The Heywood-Wakefield cabinet is of woven reed and cane. This construction would add value and, of course, to many serious collectors the Heywood-Wakefield name is prestigious since the company is associated with top quality products.

A reed crib suspended on a frame so that it swings is a rare item. Its round inverted crown at the top had a purpose. Mosquitos and flies and other insects were prevalent and could bite baby. To combat this a net could be draped from the crown to cover the bed. The style is gentle. Scrolls (some call them curlicues) were not used as decorations much before 1893, and this type of cradle was available around 1880.

A baby carrier with a dual purpose is unusual. This one is made of German reed and has retractable wheels so it also could be used as a carriage. It dates to the late 1800s.

Raggedy Andy™ seems to be enjoying his ride in the tiny sulky, but he can't invite Raggedy Ann™ to join him because a sulky offers elite seating for only one person. This product of late last century has double handles as if it were meant to be hitched to a beast or burden. It is made of willow and bentwood.

Sulky, 26" long, 9" wide, 13" high, **$145.**

This late 1800s sewing rocker of German reed has an unusual pattern of pierced loops that form the back slats. A ball and stick motif, birdcage designs on the wrapped upright posts, and scrolls add to the decorative effect. While the chair is unusual, the small lidded sewing basket beside it is found more readily since it is from this century.

A somewhat similar design is included on the fancy rocker, its arms terminating in a scroll. In addition to balls and sticks and scrolls, the back is enhanced by a panel of spider web cane. The seat is of pressed cane, and posts and rungs are wrapped. It also is from the late 1800s.

Rocker with ball and stick design, upholstered seats, 18½″ wide, 43½″ high, **$375.**

Rocker, 22″ arm to arm, 39″ high, **$350.**

This wicker work stand fulfills the Art Nouveau (later 1800s, early 1900s) desire for fluid curves and many flowers.

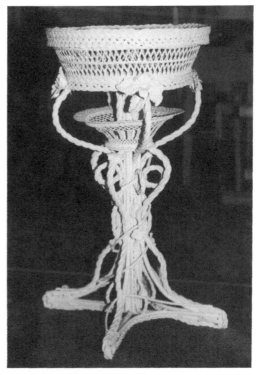

Work stand, Art Nouveau, 14½″ top diameter, 26″ high, **$395.**

The graceful delicate lines of this unique *folding table* are appealing. A basket of flowers is the central design in the wooden top with its outline of wicker work. It is from the early 1900s.

Wicker chandeliers are not readily obtainable. The collectors who own this one were so excited and delighted to acquire it that they hung their new purchase immediately so that it could make its modeling debut in this book.

Reception chairs are possible to find, but are uncommon. They were popular props in photography studios in the late 1800s and early 1900s. A panel of spider web caning, many scrolls, and birdcage designs on the upright post and the front rung contribute to produce an elegant appearance. The picture of a lad posing back in 1910 was picked up at an antique show. He looks as if he found the ornate chair a bit stiff.

Folding table, 24″ diameter, 26″ high, **$225.**

Chandelier, 20″ diameter, 22″ high, **$300.**

Photographer's chair with 7-year-old boy. Photo taken in 1910.

116

Photographer's chair, 33" wide, 18" deep, 42" high, **$650.**

Lingerie stand, 17" square, 24½" high, **$175.**

A wicker lingerie stand is not an easy item to acquire. Its bins pivot out or can be pushed in to form a rectangular stand. It is not an early wicker item, but an interesting one.

Muffin stands in tiers are unusual also. The weave suggests a 1920s product.

Muffin stand, 36" high, **$255.**

Towel rack, 24" wide, 7" deep, 16" high, **$85.**

The mirror for this shelf-towel rack combination has been removed because the owners want to have it resilvered. In the early 1900s running water was not available in many small town and rural homes. A basin was filled from the well for washing at meal times. A towel hung ready on a little rack in the kitchen. Wicker racks were not common, however.

Comb cases were kept nearby so that a person could "tidy up." Most were of tin, so it is unusual to find a woven one.

Comb case, 13" wide, 14" high, **$55**

Woven top hat, 13″ diameter, 6″ high, **$45.**

Circa 1925 is the date a dealer places on this woven hat. It's a fun item and a bit different.

All the articles in this chapter don't rate a "rare" tag. Some may not be even medium rare, but they are wicker items that are not readily available.

Deep-skirted ottoman, 19″ square, 17″ high, **$175.**

Two-piece matched set; chair, 21″ arm to arm, 33″ high; ottoman, 23″ wide, 20″ deep, 18″ high. **Set: $600.**

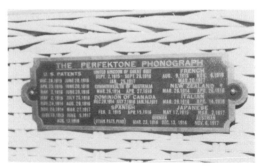

The Perfektone Phonograph metal label found on the Heywood Wakefield phonograph case showing first U. S. patent date of Dec. 28, 1915.

Heywood Wakefield phonograph case from Manley, Iowa, museum; 17″ wide, 21″ deep, 16″ high. No available price.

Game table, 36″ square, 30″ high, **$475.** Finger-hold chairs, 32″ high; set of four chairs, **$160 each.**

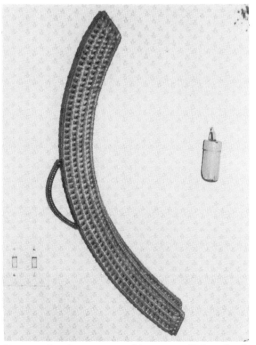

Buggy wheel cover, used to cover dirty wheels so women's long skirts wouldn't get dirty when they got in and out of the carriage; 28″ tip to tip, 2¾″wide, **$125.**

Victorian single-bed headboard, 36″ wide, 50″ high, **$125.**

8 Walking in a Wicker Wonderland

"How can my brother, the former football player, possibly co-exist with fragile antiques?" his sister asked incredulously.

The wife of the athletic male gently replied, "My husband and I have a thing about wicker. We have about seventy pieces. Our whole house is decorated with it."

She added that they hope to upgrade gradually, selling their common pieces to acquire more elaborate furnishings. Their inventory already includes unusual items tastefully displayed. Actually, the ex-football player fits comfortably into their domestic decor and is anxious to seek out more wicker to enjoy. Maybe the coined term "wickerator" for a decorator who specializes in wicker is applicable to this house. Woven articles prevail throughout.

Although in many homes woven furniture is confined to one room, a porch, or patio, the occupants of another cheerful home we toured found wicker comfortable and compatible throughout. Walking in a wicker wonderland that features "settings" of woven furniture may help others see its possibilities.

Turn back in time to the last century. An 1874 list of products produced by the Wakefield Rattan Company includes the item "wicker clothes beater." That household tool dates to an era when it was rude, crude and disgustingly sensual to utter "leg." Indeed, a man was delighted if he caught a glimpse of a lady's ankle as she raised her floor-sweeping skirt to enter a buggy or to avoid street mud. Those yards of flowing goods she wore daily must have gathered much dust. Washing clothes by hand was an arduous task, despite the possible assistance of a "hired girl." Besides, there must have been dress materials that did not wash well. Plus the drying! In inclement weather clothes were hung inside to dry. If a summer were damp, a mustiness prevailed. Hand wrung

Wicker beater in wall grouping, 31″ long, **$52.**

Center table with wooden top and "Eiffel Tower" base, 44″ diameter, 29½″ high, **$600.**

Victorian armchair with high back, 28″ arm to arm, 45″ high, **$725.** Victorian corner chair with 68 balls and 48 curlicues, 31″ arm to arm, 38″ high, **$825.**

materials hung heavy with wetness. Was it the women's clothes that required the beaters? Male pants and coats must have acquired a film after repeated buggy rides over dirt roads. This causes one to wonder if the smaller-sized wicker tools currently tagged "rug beater" could possibly be clothes beaters instead. There was a need for some such dry cleaning. Currently beaters are used as part of wall groupings, their original purpose ignored. Vacuum cleaners have eliminated the need to drag rugs outdoors and flop them over clothes lines or fences while someone flayed them

furiously every spring housecleaning time. At any rate, by adding interest to a wall, beaters again are being utilized.

Woven furniture looks dressed up in this formal "parlor," which peeks back into the past by way of the walnut tufted chair in the right background and the ornamental Willets Manufacturing Company vase in the center of the table.

Another picture shows how attractive and inviting wicker furniture can be when arranged enchantingly.

Sofa, 72″ wide, 24″ deep, 30″ high, **$450.** Coffee table, 37″ wide, 22½″ deep, 18″ high, **$175.** Round lamp table, 24″ diameter, 30″ high, **$165.** Lamp, 28″ high, **$85.** Sofa, coffee table, and lamp circa 1960; round lamp table circa 1920.

Plant stand, 28″ wide, 11″ deep, 31″ high, **$110.** Lady's side chair, 22″ arm to arm, 38″ high, **$245.** Basket with gesso roses, 11″ diameter, 12″ high, **$55.** Bar Harbor armchair, 28″ arm to arm, 35″ high, **$310.**

Baby buggy, 49″ long, 17½″ deep, 40½″ high, **$225.**

This porch setting could be as homey inside as it is out. The suite came complete with a sofa, two chairs, the coffee table, and the lamp and was sold at about the time of the revival of interest in wicker furniture (1960s).

A bedroom with a lacy iron bed has a soft feminine appearance when combined with a wicker baby buggy and delicate fabrics.

A sun porch fits its name. The hanging basket and the planter box provide a bright look.

Hanging basket, **$45;** plant box, **$55.**

Sofa table, 60″ long, 18″ wide, 30″ high, **$250.** Table lamp should have silk insert, 20″ high, shade diameter, 18″, **$210.** Lemonade caddy, **$90.** Plant stand, 43″ high, 14″ diameter, **$160.**

Armchair at left, 23″ arm to arm, 36″ high, **$310.** Armchair at right, 22″ arm to arm, 31″ high, **$295.** Footstool with turned wooden legs (a compatible piece with Wicker), 25″ wide, 15″ deep, 17″ high, **$160.**

A long table would receive its name by its choice of companionship. Behind a davenport it would be called a sofa table. One with a base shelf has a purpose. It would hold reading materials and would be referred to as a library table.

A half-round table serves at the end of a sofa. Bright upholstery material reminiscent of cretonne, the common fabric in the 1920-30 period, covers the sofa's seat cushion.

Sofa, 58″ long, 31¼″ high, **$475.** Half-round end table, Heywood-Wakefield, 24″ wide, 12″ deep, 24″ high, **$210.**

Three-piece matching chair, footstool and rocker: chair, 24″ arm to arm, 36″ high; footstool, 22″ wide, 25″ deep, 18″ high; rocker, 24″ arm to arm, 35″ high. **Set: $1,100.**

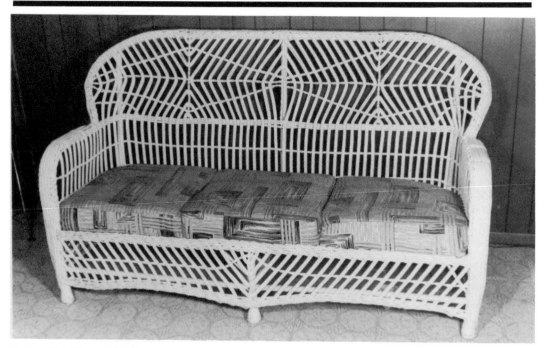

Sofa, 65″ wide, 37″ high, **$400.**

For comparison, here are two look-alike sofas that were photographed in different cities. Each has its own personality — one serves in a recreational area, and the other dresses up a living room.

Sofa, 65″ wide, 37″ high, **$400.**

A clever counter setup in a bathroom displays childhood items. The miniature cradle contains individual soaps for guests. The baby scale with its wicker basket top might hold a fresh supply of hand towels. Blocks are built up on the left. One woman spelled out "welcome" with her old-time wooden letters.

Patent (platform) rocker, 25″ wide, 47″ high, **$525**. Floor lamp, 73″ high, shade 22½″ diameter, **$550**. Smoking stand with brass tray, 28½″ high, **$110**. Footstool, 14″ wide, 10″ deep, 9″ high, **$145**.

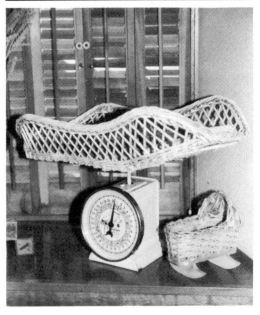

Baby scales, 23″ long, 5″ high, **$95**. Toy cradle, 7″ long, 7″ high, **$65**.

The patent (platform) rocker in this setting has rolled (or serpentine) arms, scrolls (curlicues), and open work in the back and apron. A floor lamp is ready to spread its light. For the family smoker, a stand that includes an ashtray is readily available. The footstool is a specialty of the house — the owner wove hair from the family dog and her own homespun wool together to form a herringbone pattern. The top of the stool was upholstered with this material.

Bringing the outdoors in is the responsibility of these baskets with trailing vines that vibrate with color. A square planter to the rear assists.

Three baskets (left to right): 27″ high, **$35**; 42″ high, **$45**; 27″ high, **$40**.

Move into the boudoir. The only wicker beds found available to photograph were "not old" and are not included. However, a touch from the past coordinated them with other furnishings that are. Frequently, in days of yore, a feminine touch was added to wicker by tying dainty ribbons on it. A modern-day housewife knew this and her white twin beds with heart-shaped head-boards have delicate red bows entwined in them. Red and white print curtains hang at the windows and rag dolls in chairs or buggies add their comfortable colors to create a young girl's room. A happy valentine setting emerges from this creative approach to home decorating.

In one bedroom a chaise longue is enhanced with the addition of quilts of many colors.

Another inviting chaise has pockets for magazines or sewing materials.

Chaise longue with magazine holders, 54" long, 33" wide, **$750.**

There are two chairs pulled up near this table as if inviting family members to sit for a sip of coffee or a bite to eat. Perhaps many word or card games were played here.

Chaise longue, 65" long, 27½" wide, 38½" high at head, **$625.**

Round table, 43" diameter, 29" high, **$550.** Chair, 34" high, **$110.**

This attractive desk and chair were in need of repairs when acquired. Undaunted, the owner made the necessary restoration herself. Others asked for aid for their ailing wicker, and a business began and grew until a waiting list developed. The table lamp has a tight weave, and the wastebasket features floral garlands of gesso (plaster). Note the easel that peeks in at the right. Wicker easels are uncommon.

A porch support pole has been retrieved to serve as a base upon which to place "hangies." The large one-handled basket is a sought-after type. The white tray has a braided edge of wicker, and the planter box adds color.

Desk, 36″ wide, 21″ deep, 29½″ high, rail 8½″; chair, 36″ high, **$500** for the two pieces. Table lamp, 20″ high; shade diameter, 18″, **$200**. Waste basket, 12″ diameter, **$35**.

The Art Deco sewing rocker has a repaired drawer for supplies. A wicker table is topped by a basket of vines to make a homey grouping.

Basket grouping, **$35** to **$65**.

Sewing rocker, 33″ high, **$275**. Round table, 26″ diameter, 27″ high, **$175**. Basket, 16″ long, 20″ high, **$40**.

Armchair, 29″ arm to arm, 36″ high, **$250.** Sewing stand, 17″ wide, 14″ deep, 27″ high, **$250.**

The willow and rattan sewing stand and Bar Harbor type chair are a unit.

This window seat or daybed is tucked in amid a happy abundance of wicker. A plant stand is bursting with green and other pieces form a background for a wicker, wicker everywhere look.

Window seat, 78″ long, **$575.**

Sewing stand, Heywood-Wakefield, 17″ wide, 14″ deep, 26″ high, **$225.** Table lamp, 22″ high, shade diameter, 18″, **$165.**

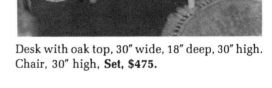

Desk with oak top, 30″ wide, 18″ deep, 30″ high. Chair, 30″ high, **Set, $475.**

A Heywood-Wakefield sewing stand featuring a base shelf with scrolls is employed as a lamp table. The lampshade has repeated swirls.

Fans and a wicker vase are on top of this rush desk. A fiber chair sits in front.

Now that you have seen how others create settings with their woven furniture, it may give you ideas so that you can enjoy walking in a wicker wonderland in your own home.

9 What's New in Wicker

For hundreds of years wicker seemed to be in hibernation until the mid-1800s, then it emerged from its prolonged Sleeping Beauty stage and became a style setter. Today, modern manufacturers are quite skillful at recreating patterns from the past at the suggestion of interior decorators. Their handwoven reincarnations of fancy Victorian chairs or sofas are expensive because they are special orders. Labor and material costs are high, but a purchaser expects to pay well for an original.

Others are developing all-new designs. One innovative creator is Danny Ho Fong of Tropi-Cal in Los Angeles, California. He uses rattan extensively. Mr. Fong's dramatic interpretations are found in handsome hotels and restaurants. The Museum of Modern Art in New York includes his wave chaise with its wrapped rattan steel frame in its permanent collection. His catalog is rich with dramatic names for his original designs: Casablanca, Indonesia, and Molokai. Mr. Fong sent Tropi-Cal's catalog in answer to a request for pictures of his work for this book.

Casablanca group by Danny Ho Fong includes sofa beds, various tables and chairs, and bar stool, pictured. Courtesy Tropi-Cal, Los Angeles.

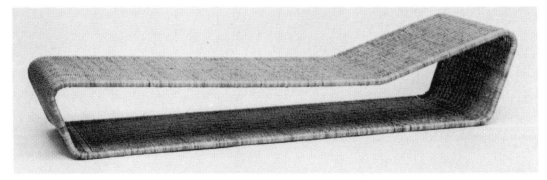

Danny Ho Fong's modern interpretation of wicker displays a wave chaise. Its steel frame is wrapped with brown rattan. Courtesy Tropi-Cal, Los Angeles.

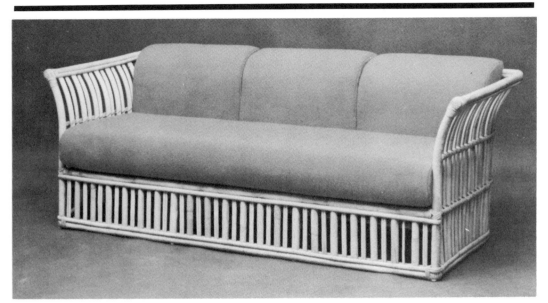

The rattan tulip sofa designed by Danny Ho Fong. Courtesy Tropi-Cal, Los Angeles.

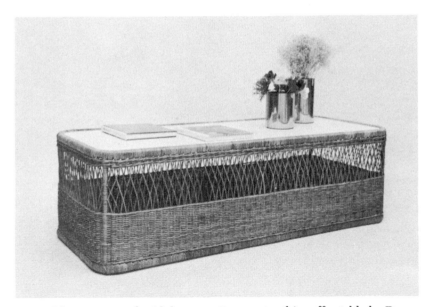

A metal frame wrapped with brown rattan creates this coffee table by Danny Ho Fong. Courtesy of Tropi-Cal, Los Angeles.

These distinctly original products are not what concern antiquers, however. The inexpensively constructed imports, frequently made to resemble Victorian ware, and the deceptions that are practiced bother collectors most. New buyers want to know, "How can I tell the old from the new?" A few clues follow:

Heft Test Erma Wilson, a woman who sells and repairs wicker, carries a new wicker lamp with her when she displays her wares at shows. If a prospective buyer questions the age of her items, she invites them to make the heft test. Her new lamp is quite light, while the old models have some weight. Most pieces that are imported from Eastern countries are woven over bamboo or rattan and are extremely light. The wooden frames of the past were made of selected hardwoods such as oak, hickory, or maple, all woods that have some weight to them. Hefting articles is one good method of determining their age.

Frizzies, Frays Quality shows. Many times recent inexpensive imports from Asiatic countries have frizzies on them — small hairlike strays from the woven material, which is not of a good grade. Frays occur when some of the loose strands that were not attached properly unwind. At times it is possible to find breaks since the material appears brittle and dry. Dryness is detrimental to reed, rush, or willow furniture.

The Staples The ends of the wrap may be stapled to the frame, or braids and scrolls may be attached in this manner. Quality wicker of recent construction would avoid these frailties, and pre-1930 American collectible examples should be of better materials.

Seat Speaks Hand woven cane goes through holes drilled in a wooden frame in the seat of a chair. The ends of pressed or pre-woven sheet cane fit into a groove in a chair's wooden frame. Reed with a horizontal over-under pattern, or later cushions with springs, formed chair bottoms. Look carefully for a wooden frame. Also, if the woven pattern is circular rather than horizontal and radiates out from the center of the seat, your chair is probably a recent import.

Comparison Shop Visit import stores and compare their wares with those available at antique shops and shows. You can see and feel the difference.

The chair illustrated is of better quality than the recent imports and dates to the 1960s. It is compatible with the collectible wicker. In style it resembles the stick reed or stick fiber furnishings produced in about 1929.

One dealer had these warnings to offer. Watch for new shades on old lamps. This

Chair, circa 1965, 32″ arm to arm, 39″ high, **$90.**

New hanging planter, 5″ wide, 12″ high, **$15.**

reduces value. Check for slight differences in weave, material, color, and for signs of wear. And new birdcages on old stands or in combination with ferneries should not be purchased without the change being explained. A customer has the right to know.

One woman said, "New items can be pretty, too." Certainly some well made objects do fit in with the old woven furniture, and it is possible to find attractive accessory articles. For example, this small hanging planter was purchased recently.

10 Care and Repair of Wicker

Was the wicker fashioned from natural or man-made materials? It is essential to know before one can care for wicker furniture properly. Mother Nature's products are easier to take care of than man-made imitations. In order to tell the difference, review the facts about materials given in Chapter One. For a rapid resume, see Chapter Four.

Washing Natural Wicker

You will need warm soapy water, a soft brush, clear rinse water, and clean cloths.

Natural rattan, reed, cane, and willow can be scrubbed gently with a brush dampened in warm soapy water and rinsed in clear tepid water. Wooden seats or framework should be wiped dry to prevent spotting. Upkeep should include occasional dustings with a damp cloth.

If the pieces creak and groan, they are mournfully singing, "Nobody knows how dry I am." A hose-applied bath outside could prove beneficial.

Man-made fiber of twisted treated paper and sea grasses do not tolerate water, and hosing or scrubbing would be detrimental. They can be cleaned with a slightly moistened rag and wiped dry.

Removing Paint

Spring housecleaning time in the past often meant that wicker was covered with a fresh coat of paint and layers built up. The restorers consulted do not recommend dipping wicker in a tank to strip it of color. It may be old, brittle and could fray. Instead, they suggest a more gentle approach using paint remover applied by brush as instructed by the manufacturer.

Man-made fiber and sea grasses would be damaged by paint removers.

Applying a Finish

Wicker furniture made out of natural materials is porous. Because of this, it soils easily, and it should have a protective covering. After you have let the surface dry following the paint removing and it is all clean, apply flat or gloss undercoating with a brush. This acts as a sealer to prevent over absorption. Now it is possible to spray on paint following the directions on an aerosol can. Gloss white is frequently chosen, and a thin coat should be applied with a steady spraying stream. After this dries thoroughly, repeat the process until several thin coats complete the job.

If you plan to stain the furniture, try some on the bottom, where it won't show, to be sure it is compatible and the shade you desire. If, when it dries, it is what you want, apply several thin coats, allowing for drying time between applications. Lacquer, varnish, or shellac can be sprayed in a similar manner. A small air compressor with sprayer could be utilized instead of the aerosol can.

Repairing Wicker

A novice will not need many tools. The workshop should include:

1. Two sizes of needle-nose pliers
2. A mat knife
3. Screwdrivers
4. A spline remover with a hook on the end if you plan to remove and replace pressed (pre-woven) cane webbing on seats.
5. Clamps for gluing
6. Hammer
7. Scissors
8. Clippers
9. Chisel

Supplies include:

1. White glue because it doesn't show
2. Rags for wiping off excess glue or other jobs
3. Tongue depressors to spread glue
4. Wedges

It is a good idea to send a sample of any repair materials you need to the supplier and ask him to ship the required supplies. For example, there are four sizes of rush and five of cane, reed can be flat or oval and sea grasses come in two sizes, etc.

It is almost impossible to tell someone how to tie a shoe. It is much better to show a person, and then let him or her try until the task is completed. One restorer stated that this is also the best way to learn how to repair wicker. Watch someone. Then participate yourself, learning as you go along.

Some restorers feel there are various ways to complete the same mending project. Consider how the end product looks. How you get there depends on individual taste, and one way can be as good as another.

Wrapping Repairs

You will need:
1. White glue
2. Binding cane
3. Scissors
4. Wet cloths to wipe off excess glue

Soak the binding cane in warm water for a few minutes until it is flexible. When wrapping is missing from the leg of a chair, turn the chair upside down so the leg can be reached easily. Run a line of glue down the leg and apply some to one end of the soaked cane. Slip the end up under the existing wrap to catch it. When it is secure, wrap the binding cane snugly around and around the leg until the bare space is filled in. Apply white glue to the end and tuck it in through the rounds you have just completed. Wipe off any excess glue with a damp cloth.

It was a set of six decrepit chairs that lured one couple into the repair business. In her endeavor to rehabilitate them, the woman took the chairs and isolated herself in a room. Almost with microscopic eyes, she examined their damaged surfaces until she determined how the chairs were woven and the assistance they would require to overcome their ailing, frail appearance. After that she was ready to set to work. Later, the completed set was sold for a profit, and she and her husband were in business. In the same manner, if you seek a do-it-yourself job, study your piece of furniture until you are aware of its lines and faults.

Replacing Spokes

You will need:
1. Soaked reed the size of the existing good spokes
2. A clipping tool
3. White glue
4. A damp cloth to wipe off excess glue

Soak the reed approximately five minutes, depending on its thickness — thicker reeds require slightly more soaking time. Spokes are the vertical woven supports on the back of a wicker chair that are interwoven with horizontal reeds. Cut out a broken spoke three or four rows above where the horizontal reed is woven around it. Do the same at the bottom of the spoke. Insert the reed in the bottom weave where the damaged one was cut away. Following the existing pattern, meander this new reed up through the design to the top. Bend the reed slightly as you work, so it can be inserted in the top weave where the broken one was removed. Sometimes this job is easier if the reed is cut to a point at the end. Glue may be added if desired.

When more than one spoke needs to be replaced, the place in the weave where they are inserted should be staggered for strength. For example, go under four rows of the horizontal with one spoke, perhaps two with another, and five with another so that all do not begin and end in the same horizontal row.

One repairer warns — do not soak the reed too long. You don't want it too pliable or flabby — that makes it hard to work with. It should be just wet enough to bend without breaking.

Replacing Horizontals

The horizontal weave generally follows an over/under pattern, and replacing it is done in much the same manner as the spokes are replaced. Cut out the damaged section back of the spoke. Again, study how to match the existing woven design and, using a soaked reed of the required length, duplicate the pattern. Finish by tucking the two ends of the new reed under the cut-off ends of the old reed. Glue for added strength.

Installing a Pressed Cane Seat

When a groove runs all the way around the wooden frame in a chair, it has a set-in (or pressed) cane bottom. The material is pre-woven in sheets and may be referred to as webbing. Most wicker cane sets were done in this manner and not caned by hand. You will need:

1. A spline remover with a hooked end or a screwdriver
2. A hammer
3. A wide chisel
4. Clippers
5. White glue
6. A mat knife
7. A wooden wedge
8. Pre-soaked woven sheet cane, called webbing or pressed cane, cut several inches larger than the hole in the chair seat
9. Soaked spline cut about an inch longer than required (spline comes in different sizes and is the triangular reed that fits into the groove)
10. Two pieces of spline about 1″ in length to temporarily hold the cane tightly in place
11. A tongue depressor to spread the glue
12. Damp rag

Most of these articles are available through supply houses. A wicker worker states that the spline remover with the hooked end works well, but a straight end does not.

The first step is to remove the damaged seat and clean out the groove. Set the chisel on the inside edge of the spline and tap it carefully with the hammer all the way around the seat. Repeat on the outer edge of the spline. After loosening the spline in this manner, pry it up with the screwdriver or the hooked spline remover. Be careful not to damage the wood. Scrape out any hardened glue so the new will adhere well.

The restorer interviewed felt the webbing should soak six to eight hours. Cut the spline to meet the size required by the chair, plus a little extra, perhaps an inch. Select a thickness that will fit into the groove with ease so that it can be taken out with your fingers. Soak the spline about fifteen minutes just prior to use. Wipe off excess moisture. Square seats require four strips of spline, one for each side. A rounded one needs a continuous piece to match the circumference of the seat.

Position the cane webbing over the seat so that there is about an inch extra on each side. There is a wrong side and a right side to cane — the shiny side goes up. Gently force the cane down into the groove at the rear of the chair by tapping the top of the wedge with your hammer. Secure temporarily with an inch piece of spline inserted over the cane in the groove. Be sure the pattern is straight as you pull the cane snugly to the front of the seat and temporarily secure it in the same manner. It should be taut and straight. Now go around the entire seat carefully, tapping the cane into the groove. The excess will stick out. Remove the two temporary holders. Pour white glue into the groove, spreading it around with a tongue depressor. Tap the wedge with a hammer to get the pre-soaked spline into the groove on top of the cane. Go completely around the seat. On round chair bottoms, cut the spline so the ends butt together. On square ones the ends of the four strips should meet exactly at the corners. After the spline is securely in place, cut off the excess cane with a mat knife. Repeat the wedge tapping process around the chair spline to insure that the spline and the seat frame are even. Work more glue into each side of the spline to insure a lasting bond. Use a damp cloth to wipe off excess glue. Set the chair aside for at least two days to dry thoroughly at room temperature before using it.

Remember such materials as sea grasses, paper rush, and man-made twisted paper fiber are to be soaked. Water damages them.

These are rudimentary repairs. Good luck.

Wicker Shops, Suppliers

Here are five shops that specialize in wicker furniture.

> The Antique Repair Shop
> (Vic and Anne Durkin)
> 7222 Magoun Avenue
> Hammond, Indiana 46324
> (By appointment only)

> Antique Wicker & Collectibles
> (Pat Hill)
> 1038 - 3rd Ave., S. E.
> Cedar Rapids, Iowa 52403

> Grandma's Attic & Wicker Works
> (Vicki Dahlstrom)
> 301 West Third St.
> Milan, Illinois 61264

> Wanna Buy a Duck
> (David and Carroll Swope)
> 805 McKinley Avenue N.W.
> Canton, Ohio 44703

> Wilson Wicker & Weaving
> (John and Erma Wilson)
> 1509 Main Street
> Cedar Falls, Iowa 50613

All shared helpful information that is included in the text. Dahlstrom, Durkins and Wilsons offer efficient repair services to the public, but the Swopes do restoration only on their own pieces. If you are in doubt about repair shops selected from the yellow pages of the telephone book, visit them and inspect samples of their work in order to determine their restoration skills.

It is better to purchase structurally sound articles. If the frame itself is bad, this entails extensive labor. Any hand work is costly. If you cannot do the restoration yourself, try to be sure your selections are well preserved. This may save you money in the long run.

Two reliable suppliers were contacted and agreed to be listed in this book.

> WSI Distributors
> 1165 First Capitol Drive
> P.O. Box 1235
> St. Charles, Missouri 63301
> 1-314-946-5811

WSI Distributors carries a complete line of caning and weaving materials. A catalog that includes its other merchandise is available for $2.

> The Wise Company
> P.O. Box 118
> 6503 St. Claude Avenue
> Arabi, Louisiana 70032
> 1-504-277-7551

Wise sells cane webbing and strand cane, fiber rush, seagrass, flat and oval reed, and flat paper splints. Its two-volume catalog costs $3.50. Both are fall, 1982, prices.

Glossary

Apron a piece that hides the construction details on chairs, tables, and chests. On a chair, it is under the seat. An apron on a table is beneath the top where the legs connect.

Art Nouveau an arts and crafts movement begun in about 1895 characterized by the use of flowing curves and designs from nature such as youthful curved feminine figures, flowers, insects, and butterflies. This style was used into the early 1900s.

Art Deco the name came from an exposition held in Paris in 1925. Geometric designs were emphasized, and the Art Deco influence was felt in the late 1920s through the 1930s. The diamond design on wicker is called Art Deco even though it was in use prior to 1925.

ball and stick as the name implies, a ball with a stick through it was used as an ornamental device on furniture.

Bar Harbor an open weave design that became popular in the early 1900s to reduce the cost of hand labor. Since many rockers were used on the verandas of resort hotels, the name Bar Harbor was attached to those with an open lattice-work.

binding cane this is wider and thicker cane that was frequently used as a wrap on wicker furniture. It often covered legs and rungs in a spiral fashion.

birdcage design this Victorian design resembles a Japanese lantern. Vertical reeds bow out to cage structural parts such as legs in a fancy manner.

braiding three long strands of reed or fiber were interwoven to form a design that hid the rough edges where the weave ended on wicker furniture. It looks like a hair style young girls have who wear their hair in braids.

cane long strip of rattan used to weave chair backs and seats.

cane webbing see webbing.

cathedral back a chair back that roughly comes to a point in the center.

circa an approximate date, such as circa 1880 (around 1880).

curlique scrolls a coiled circle design made of reed. Used on many Victorian wicker pieces, usually after 1893 and on into the early 1900s.

fan backs a design used in the back of chairs that resembled a hand fan. Other designs such as banjos and hearts appeared also.

fiber man-made twisted, treated paper. Also called fibre, art fiber, fiber reed, or fiber rush. Invented in the early 1900s. By the late 1920s it was used more than natural reed in the construction of wicker furniture.

geometric designs circles, squares, diamonds, triangles, and the like used as designs in furniture. This was a popular Art Deco concept, circa 1925 on into the 1930s.

gesso molded plaster of Paris designs sometimes found on wicker as an added decoration. Floral designs were often used. Around 1910.

horizontal a weave that goes crosswise rather than up and down (vertical).

Lloyd's loom patented in 1917. It wove man-made fiber in sheets that were attached to standard frames to make wicker furniture. Since it could do the work of thirty men, this tightly woven product soon dominated the indusry.

Mission a style of furniture with boxy, straight, practical lines that was introduced around 1900 and opposed Victorian fancy circles and ornate designs. Popular for about twenty years, it is now being revived.

natural wicker not painted. It may have a coating of stain, lacquer, shellac, or varnish to protect its surface from soiling. A collector usually values natural wicker, and it is often higher in price than painted pieces.

osiers pliant twigs from willow trees that are used to make wicker furniture.

patent, platform rockers two names for rocking chairs that were fastened to a base by coil springs.

prairie, sea grasses dried, long, strong grasses that had a ropelike appearance when twisted or a floating feel when used as free strands. May be used for panels, bulb-feet wrap or for a shelf or small piece of wicker furniture.

pressed cane seat a seat made of prewoven cane and set in a wooden frame by forcing the ends into a groove.

prewoven cane see webbing

rattan a strong, tall, slender, vine-like palm that bends well without breaking and is used to make wicker furniture.

reed the inner part or pith of rattan, originally considered waste material. First used in the 1850s to make wicker furniture. It soon became the most popular material in use until man-made fiber replaced it in the 1920s.

roll sometimes called serpentine. A hollow roll edge found on the backs and arms of late Victorian and early 1900 wicker furniture. Snake-like, it sometimes extends down under the seat of chairs also.

rush a perennial swamp plant whose stems are used to make woven objects such as baskets and chair seats. Today much rush is man-made of spiral paper.

scroll name found in old catalogs for curlicue. See curlicue.

sea grasses see prairie grasses.

serpentine see roll.

set-in cane seat see pressed cane

sheet cane see pressed cane

spider web cane a fancy woven cane design used in panels in the back of chairs. Its intricate pattern resembles a spider web.

spline a triangular reed used to hold the edges of a pressed cane or set-in cane seat in the grooves in the chair frame.

spoke the vertical reeds that support the horizontal weave in furniture. For example, the reeds go up and down and a pattern can be formed with a crosswise weave.

Victorian the period (1837-1901) when England's Queen Victoria reigned. Much of the furniture made during this era was ornate.

webbing pre-woven sheets of cane used to make pressed cane or set-in cane seats. See pressed cane seat.

wicker the generic or family name for furniture made from materials such as rattan, cane, reed, willow, sea and prairie grasses, rush, and fiber. Old catalogs refer to rattan, reed, or fiber products. The name "wicker" came into use around 1900.

willow see osiers. Flexible twigs from certain willow trees used to make woven products.

Bibliography

Corbin, Patricia. *All about Wicker*. New York: E.P. Dutton, 1978.

Shirley, G.E. *Great Grandmother's Wicker Furniture 1880s–1920s*. Burlington, Iowa: Craftsman Press.

Saunders, Richard. *Collecting & Restoring Wicker Furniture*. New York: Crown Publishers, Inc., 1976.

Thompson, Frances. *The Complete Wicker Book*. Des Moines, Iowa: Wallace-Homestead Book Co., 1978.

Weiss, Jeffrey. *Cornerstone Collector's Guide to Wicker*. New York: Cornerstone Library, Simon & Schuster, 1981.

Index

About the Authors

Bob and Harriett Swedberg especially enjoy collecting antiques because of the fine friendships they have made with others who share this interest. This hobby links the generations, binds various nationalities together, and spans economic barriers. The Swedbergs like to share their knowledge through teaching classes, conducting seminars, lecturing, and exhibiting items at antiques shows. They have written columns including "Antique Echoes" in *Collectors Journal* and have been featured guests on many radio and television programs. These Moline, Illinois, residents are available for programs.